D0838519

Volume V
The Civil Rights Movement and the Vietnam Era
(1964–1975)

The Twentieth Century

The Progressive Era and
the First World War
(1900–1918)

The Roaring Twenties and
an Unsettled Peace
(1919–1929)

The Great Depression
and World War II
(1930–1945)

Postwar Prosperity
and the Cold War
(1946–1963)

The Civil Rights Movement
and the Vietnam Era
(1964–1975)

Baby Boomers and the
New Conservatism
(1976–1991)

Volume V
The Civil Rights Movement and the Vietnam Era
(1964–1975)

Editorial Consultants

Matthew T. Downey, University of California at Berkeley

Harvey Green, Northeastern University

David M. Katzman, University of Kansas

Ruth Jacknow Markowitz, SUNY College at Oswego

Albert E. Moyer, Virginia Polytechnic Institute

Macmillan Publishing Company

New York

Maxwell Macmillan Canada

Toronto

Editorial Credits

Developed and produced by Visual Education Corporation, Princeton, N.J.

Project Editor: Richard Bohlander

Associate Project Editor: Michael Gee

Writers: Linda Barrett, Cathie Cush, Galen Guengerich, Lois Markham, Donna Singer

Editors: Risa Cottler, Susan Garver, Amy Lewis, Linda Scher, Betty Shanley, Bonnie Swaim, Frances Wiser

Production Supervisor: Mary Lyn Sodano

Inputting: Cindy Feldner

Interior Design: Maxson Crandall

Cover Design: Mike McIver

Layout: Maxson Crandall, Lisa Evans, Graphic Typesetting Service, Elizabeth Onorato

Photo Research: Cynthia Cappa, Sara Matthews

Maps: Parrot Graphics

Graphs: Virtual Media

Proofreading Management: Amy Davis

Photo Credits

AP/Wide World Photos: 49

Archive Photos: 86

Archive Photos/Central Press: 113 (left)

Archive Photos/London Daily Express: 3 (2nd from left), 34

Bettmann/Hulton: 117 (left)

Courtesy of Intel Corporation: 85

Courtesy of the Vietnam News Agency, Hanoi: 55

Henri Bureau/Sygma: 61

NASA: 3 (4th from left), 74, 78, 79

Photofest: 92 (left), 101, 102

Simon Fraser/Custom Medical Stock Photo: 84

The Bettmann Archive: 45 (left)

United Press International Photo: 20, 67

UPI/Bettmann: 3 (3rd from left; far right), 12, 16, 18, 21, 23, 25, 26, 27 (right), 28, 29, 36, 37, 40, 42 (left), 43, 45 (right), 46, 52, 54, 57, 58, 60, 64, 66, 69, 71, 72, 73, 77 (both), 80, 81, 87, 90, 91, 92 (right), 94, 95, 98, 99, 103, 104, 107, 108, 111 (left), 113 (right), 114, 115, 116, 117 (right)

UPI/Bettmann Newsphotos: 3 (far left; 5th from left), 10, 19, 27 (center; left), 30, 32, 33, 42 (right), 44, 53, 82, 88, 93, 109, 110, 111 (right)

Washington Post: 50

Macmillan Publishing Company
866 Third Avenue
New York, NY 10022

Maxwell Macmillan Canada, Inc.
1200 Eglinton Avenue East, Suite 200
Don Mills, Ontario M3C 3N1

Macmillan Publishing Company is part of the Maxwell Communication Group of Companies

Printed in the United States of America

printing number
1 2 3 4 5 6 7 8 9 10

Library of Congress Cataloging-in-Publication Data

The twentieth century / consultants, Matthew T. Downey . . . [et al.].
     p.   cm.
    Includes index.
    Contents: v. 1. The Progressive Era and the First World War (1900–1918)—v. 2. The Roaring Twenties and an Unsettled Peace (1919–1929)—v. 3. The Great Depression and World War II (1930–1945)—v. 4. Postwar Prosperity and the Cold War (1946–1963)—v. 5. The Civil Rights Movement and the Vietnam Era (1964–1975)—v. 6. Baby Boomers and the New Conservatism (1976–1991).
    ISBN 0-02-897442-5 (set : alk. paper)
    1. History, Modern—20th century. I. Downey, Matthew T.
D421.T88 1992
909.82—dc20   91-40862

Preface

The Twentieth Century is a six-book series covering the major developments of the period, from a primarily American perspective. This is the chronicle of a century unlike any before, one in which the pace of change has accelerated to the point that it is almost overwhelming.

As the century draws to a close, with such major ongoing events as the end of the Cold War and the seeming collapse of communism, it is appropriate to step back from the furious rush forward and examine the significance of the many changes we have seen in what may be the most momentous epoch in the history of the world.

Here, then, is the story of a world transformed by technology: by radio, television, and satellite communications; by automobiles, airplanes, and space travel; by antibiotics, organ transplants, and genetic engineering; by the atomic bomb; by the computer. These are just a few of the advances that have revolutionized the workings of the world and our daily lives.

Here also is the story of a century of history strongly influenced by individuals: Vladimir Lenin and Mao Ze-dong; Franklin Delano Roosevelt, Winston Churchill, and Adolf Hitler; Lech Walesa and Mikhail Gorbachev; Mohandas Gandhi and Martin Luther King Jr.; Theodore Roosevelt, John F. Kennedy, and Ronald Reagan. All have been featured actors in the drama of our times, as conveyed by these pages.

Above all else, it is the story of an American century, one in which a young democratic nation emerged as the world's most powerful force. Through two bitter world wars and an enduring cold war, the dominant influence of the United States on twentieth-century world history and culture is undeniable.

It is the story of the many forces that have transformed the face of our nation from a primarily rural, agricultural society dominated by white people of European heritage to a modern urban, industrialized, and multicultural nation. It is a story of the challenges, successes, and failures that have accompanied these fundamental changes.

Each book of this series focuses on a distinct era of the century. The six titles in the series are:

*The Progressive Era and
the First World War (1900–1918)*

*The Roaring Twenties and
an Unsettled Peace (1919–1929)*

*The Great Depression
and World War II (1930–1945)*

*Postwar Prosperity
and the Cold War (1946–1963)*

*The Civil Rights Movement
and the Vietnam Era (1964–1975)*

*Baby Boomers and the
New Conservatism (1976–1991)*

Each book is divided into six units: The Nation, The World, Business and Economy, Science and Technology, Arts and Entertainment, and Sports and Leisure. The second page of each unit includes a Datafile presenting significant statistical information in both table and graph format. All units include boxed features and sidebars focusing on particular topics of interest.

Additional features of each book include a graphic timeline of events of the period called Glimpses of the Era; a compilation of quotes, headlines, slogans, and literary extracts called Voices of the Era; a glossary of terms; a list of suggested readings; and a complete index.

The series is illustrated with historical photos, as well as original maps, graphs, and tables conveying pertinent statistical data.

Contents

GLIMPSES OF THE ERA

Feb. 12   The Beatles perform on *Ed Sullivan Show*

May 30   City of New Orleans retires last streetcar from service

July 3   Civil Rights Act passed

Aug. 4   Bodies of three civil rights workers discovered near Philadelphia, Mississippi

Aug. 7   Gulf of Tonkin Resolution passed by Congress

Dec. 10   Martin Luther King Jr. wins Nobel Peace Prize

▶ 1964

1965 ◀

Feb. 21   Black Muslim leader Malcolm X assassinated

Mar. 21–25   Civil rights march from Selma to Montgomery, Alabama, begins

June 3   Edward White II becomes first American to walk in space

Aug. 6   Voting Rights Act passed

Nov. 10   Power restored after worst electrical failure in history blacks out 7 states in U.S. and Ontario, Canada, for 2 days

May 1   U.S. planes begin bombing of Cambodia

June 13   In *Miranda v. Arizona,* Supreme Court upholds rights of criminal suspects

Sept. 6   Birth control advocate Margaret Sanger dies

Nov. 8   Edward Brooke elected first black senator in 85 years

Dec. 15   Walt Disney dies

▶ 1966

1967 ◀

Jan. 15   Green Bay Packers beat Kansas City Chiefs in first Super Bowl game

Jan. 18   Albert DeSalvo, the "Boston Strangler," sentenced to life in prison

Oct. 21–22   Peace demonstrators march on Pentagon

Nov. 7   President Johnson signs Public Broadcasting Act, establishing public television and radio

Nov. 13   *Hair* premieres in New York City

Jan. 30   Tet offensive begins

Mar. 31   President Johnson announces he will not run for reelection

Apr. 4   Martin Luther King Jr. assassinated

June 5   Robert F. Kennedy assassinated

Aug. 21   Czechoslovakia invaded by Warsaw Pact troops

Nov. 5   Shirley Chisholm elected first black Congresswoman

▶ 1968

1969 ◀

Jan. 20   Richard Nixon becomes 37th president

Feb. 8   *Saturday Evening Post* prints final issue

June 8   President Nixon announces U.S. troops to begin leaving Vietnam

June 9   Senate confirms Warren E. Burger as chief justice of Supreme Court

July 20   U.S. astronauts land on moon

Aug. 15–17   Woodstock Music and Art Fair held

GLIMPSES OF THE ERA

Apr. 22	First Earth Day celebrated
May 4	Four students killed at Kent State University in Ohio by National Guard troops during antiwar protest
May 15	First female Army generals named by President Nixon
Sept. 18	Rock musician Jimi Hendrix found dead from sleeping pill overdose
Dec. 2	Environmental Protection Agency established

► **1970**

Mar. 24	Cult leader Charles Manson and 3 women sentenced to death for 1969 murders of 7 people in a wealthy California community
May 3	More than 7,000 antiwar demonstrators arrested in Washington, D.C.
June 13	*New York Times* begins publication of Pentagon Papers on U.S. involvement in Vietnam
July 25	26th Amendment ratified, giving 18-year-olds right to vote

1971 ◄

Jan. 2	Cigarette advertising banned from airwaves
Feb. 21–28	President Nixon visits mainland China. U.S. and China reopen diplomatic relations
June 17	Five men arrested for breaking into Democratic party headquarters in Watergate complex in Washington, D.C.
July 1	First issue of *Ms.* magazine published

► **1972**

Jan. 22	In landmark *Roe v. Wade* decision, Supreme Court overturns all state laws that deny or restrict a woman's right to obtain an abortion
Jan. 27	U.S. and Vietnam agree to cease-fire. Military draft ends
May 17	Senate Select Committee begins public hearings on Watergate
Oct. 10	Vice President Spiro Agnew resigns after evidence is uncovered of political corruption during years in Maryland politics

1973 ◄

Apr. 8	Hank Aaron hits 715th home run, breaking Babe Ruth's record
Apr. 18	OPEC lifts oil embargo against U.S.
May 24	Jazz great Duke Ellington dies
Aug. 9	Nixon resigns. Gerald Ford becomes 38th president
Sept. 8	President Ford pardons Richard Nixon
Nov. 5	Ella Grasso of Connecticut becomes first woman elected governor in her own right

► **1974**

1975 ◄

Feb. 21	John Mitchell, H. R. Haldeman, and John Ehrlichman sentenced for Watergate-related activities
Apr. 30	South Vietnam falls to communist North Vietnam
June 16	Oregon becomes first state to ban sale and use of products containing chlorofluorocarbons
July 17	Astronauts and cosmonauts shake hands in space as *Apollo 18* and *Soyuz 19* dock together in first joint U.S.-Soviet space mission

THE NATION

"We stand today on the edge of a new frontier—the frontier of the 1960s, a frontier of unknown opportunities and perils, a frontier of unfulfilled hopes and threats." These prophetic words, spoken by John F. Kennedy in 1960, proclaimed the ominous uncertainty of the 1960s. These were days when, for many people, opportunities remained unknown and hopes remained unfulfilled. The threats and perils, however, were all too real.

After Kennedy's assassination in 1963, President Lyndon Johnson envisioned the Great Society program. Johnson, a self-confident Texan, used his considerable political skill to push through Congress a program of domestic reform more extensive than any since the New Deal. The nation

AT A GLANCE

- ▶ Lyndon Johnson and the Great Society
- ▶ The Vietnam War
- ▶ The Civil Rights Movement
- ▶ Richard Nixon's Political Career
- ▶ Nixon Undone: The Watergate Scandal
- ▶ The Women's Movement
- ▶ The Counterculture

seemed well on its way to dealing with poverty and racial discrimination, the two most pressing problems of the day.

It was not to be so easy, however. Even as the Great Society and the War on Poverty took shape, the nation began to come apart. The Vietnam War, racial unrest, the civil rights movement, the women's movement, conflict between generations, a growing unease at the unchecked power of the presidency—all contributed to growing divisions among Americans. The nation had not seen so much violence at home since the beginning of the twentieth century. Many people believed that the nation's basic social and political institutions were on the verge of collapse, either from the new forces of change or from failure within.

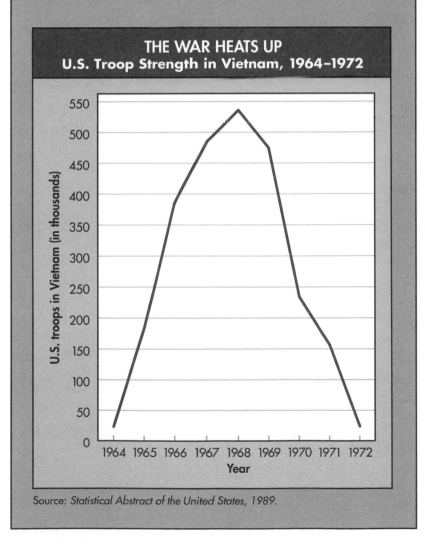

U.S. population	1960	1970
Total (in millions)	179.3	203.3
Urban	70.0%	73.5%
Rural	30.0%	26.5%
White	88.6%	87.5%
Black	10.5%	11.1%
Other	0.9%	1.4%

Social data	1964	1975
Birthrate (live births per 1,000 pop.)	21.0	14.6
Mortality rate (per 1,000 pop.)	9.4	8.8
Murder rate (per 100,000 pop.)	5.1	8.8
Persons aged 5–17 in school (per 100 pop.)	94.8	88.9

Voter turnout

1964	61.7%	1972	55.2%
1968	60.6%		

THE WAR HEATS UP
U.S. Troop Strength in Vietnam, 1964–1972

(line graph: U.S. troops in Vietnam (in thousands) on vertical axis from 0 to 550; Year on horizontal axis from 1964 to 1972. Troop strength rises from about 25 in 1964 to a peak above 535 in 1968, then declines to about 25 in 1972.)

Source: *Statistical Abstract of the United States, 1989.*

LYNDON JOHNSON AND THE GREAT SOCIETY

"My God! My God! What are we coming to?" exclaimed John McCormack, the Speaker of the House of Representatives. His exclamation was a horrified response to the shocking assassination of John F. Kennedy on November 22, 1963. The Speaker's remark was soon echoed by many other Americans. Their confidence in a bright future in which all things were possible was shattered. They feared that the tragedy of the death of their beloved president would end his dream of social change and progress for America.

Lyndon Johnson, sworn in as president aboard *Air Force One*, moved quickly to reassure a bewildered nation. "No words are strong enough to express our determination to continue the forward thrust of America that he began," he told Congress five days after the assassination. "This is no time for delay. It is a time for action."

A Bold Proposal

The tall Democrat from Texas kept his word. His political skills had been honed by 23 years of alliance-building and deal-making in Congress. He had boundless confidence in his ability to rally people to his cause—or bully them, if that became necessary. The "Johnson Treatment" became his trademark. His skillful combination of back-slapping, handshaking, and arm-twisting overwhelmed his supporters and his opponents and compelled both to put their sup-

Lyndon Johnson: The Path to Power

Lyndon Baines Johnson grew up in the hill country of central Texas, the son of a six-time member of the Texas legislature. In the Texas capital of Austin, Lyndon's father, Sam Johnson, was well known for his honesty—a rare attribute at a time when special-interest groups did most of the real governing in Texas. Because Sam Johnson was honest, however, he did not get rich in politics. As a result, Lyndon knew what life was like at "the bottom of the heap," as he said when describing his modest upbringing.

If Lyndon knew about being poor, he also knew that politicians had the power to make a difference in people's lives. He wanted to make that difference, to create a just society free of chronic poverty and hardship. The story of his journey from the hills of Texas to the White House is, more than anything else, a chronicle of the desire to succeed. High school speech teacher, U.S. representative, U.S. senator, Senate majority leader, vice president—the path to power, Johnson knew, was paved with political skill, hard work, and unswerving desire.

Most politicians of the day viewed Johnson's first campaign for Congress in 1937 as an exercise in futility. Although Johnson had served as a congressional aide in Washington, he was virtually unknown by the Texas voters. But he believed he could convince people to vote for him. Aided by his energetic wife "Lady Bird," he campaigned ceaselessly, seven days a week, up to 15 hours a day. He crisscrossed the 8,000 square miles of his vast district again and again, looking for anyone who would listen.

On the campaign trail, Johnson revealed his great strength as a politician: once you shook his hand, you were his friend. His style was simple and direct, yet insistent. On a farm or in a tiny village, Johnson reached out and grasped the voters' hands. "I'm Lyndon Johnson and I'm running for Congress," he would say, still holding on. "I want your support. I need your vote. And if you know anyone who can help me, I want to get them to help me. I need your help. Will you help me? Will you give me your helping hand?" With few exceptions, the voters of Texas's tenth congressional district did. When the results of the election were tallied, Johnson had 8,280 votes, 3,000 more than his closest opponent.

port behind Johnson and his agenda.

Johnson's crusade to create what he called the "Great Society" began by pushing through Congress Kennedy's stalled tax cut and civil rights bills. He added landmark proposals for a billion-dollar "War on Poverty" and a bold new plan for education. As Johnson campaigned for the 1964 presidential election, he explained his cause. "The Great Society rests on abundance and liberty for all. It demands an end to poverty and racial injustice." Most Americans agreed, and Johnson crushed the Republican contender, Barry Goldwater, in the November 1964 election. Voters also elected an overwhelmingly Democratic Congress. The Great Society was underway.

A Legislative Triumph

Between 1964 and 1966, Johnson worked tirelessly to reach the goals of the Great Society. His considerable powers of persuasion and a two-to-one Democratic majority in both the House and the Senate helped him achieve the most extensive program of social reform since the New Deal of the 1930s and the Fair Deal of the 1940s. Taken together, the Great Society programs constituted a stunning legislative achievement (see table). Many of these programs also had direct and lasting effects on people's lives. The number of Americans living in poverty fell from 22 percent in 1960 to 12 percent in 1969.

The Civil Rights Act of 1964 and the Voting Rights Act of 1965, for example, directed that all citizens, regardless of their race or education, be given equal access to jobs, housing, and the vote. The Economic Opportunity Act created a network of federal programs to fight poverty, an enemy that, in Johnson's words, "threatens the strength of our nation and the welfare of our people." The Medical Care Act set up Medicare and Medicaid to pay the health-care costs of elderly and poor Americans who could not afford skyrocketing medical bills. The Elementary and Secondary Education Act provided federal money to help local public and private schools handle rising costs and increased enrollments. A second education act provided federally funded scholarships for higher education.

The End of the Crusade

Putting the social programs of the Great Society into action required billions of tax dollars. Increasingly, however, the costs of the conflict in Vietnam competed for those dollars. The shortage of money, it turned out, was the least of Johnson's problems. The war in Vietnam was quickly turning into a military and political fiasco. In addition, the peaceful attempts to advance the civil rights movement met with hostile responses, and racial tensions erupted into violence. A pall of smoke hung over riot-scarred black communities across the nation.

President Johnson's ambitious dream of ending poverty and providing equal rights for all citizens was not to become reality. In 1966, Johnson lost his commanding majority in the House. By 1968, the Vietnam War had utterly destroyed the political career of the once-confident visionary from Texas.

FIRST BLACK CABINET MEMBER

Robert Clifton Weaver made history in 1966 when he was appointed secretary of the newly formed Department of Housing and Urban Development (HUD). President Johnson's appointment made him the first black Cabinet member.

After earning a Ph.D. in economics from Harvard, Weaver served in Franklin D. Roosevelt's administration, where he advised the government on black issues such as manpower, housing, and urban affairs. After World War II, Weaver taught and published several books on black and urban issues. He also worked for New York state and city housing agencies.

In 1960 President Kennedy appointed Weaver to head the federal Housing and Home Finance Agency. After serving as HUD secretary from 1966 to 1968, Weaver returned to education as a teacher and an administrator.

Launching the Great Society

Name of Legislation	Date Enacted	Purpose
Tax Reduction Act	1964	Tax-cut package meant to stimulate economic growth
Civil Rights Act	1964	Outlawed discrimination in housing and jobs; gave federal government broad power to prosecute rights abuses
Economic Opportunity Act	1964	Created Office of Economic Opportunity to begin "War on Poverty," with Head Start, Job Corps, VISTA, etc.
Wilderness Preservation Act	1965	Protected 9.1 million acres of federal forest land from development
Voting Rights Act	1965	Ended practice of requiring voters to pass literacy tests; gave federal government power to monitor registration
Immigration Act	1965	Ended immigration quotas based on racist "national origins"
Medical Care Act	1965	Established Medicare to provide health care for the elderly and Medicaid to provide health care for welfare recipients
Omnibus Housing Act	1965	Provided money for low-income housing
Elementary and Secondary Education Act	1965	Major federal aid package for education—the first in the nation's history
Higher Education Act	1965	Provided scholarships and loans for students
National Endowments for the Arts and the Humanities	1965	Provided grants for artists and the arts
Water Quality Act	1965	Required states to clean up rivers
Model Cities Act	1966	Funded slum rebuilding and mass transit
Truth in Packaging Act	1966	Set standards for labeling goods
Minimum Wage Law	1966	Raised minimum wage to $1.40 per hour
Traffic and Motor Vehicle Safety Act	1966	Established safety standards for autos and tires

THE VIETNAM WAR

After the Communists took over China in 1949, President Truman's policy of containment seemed a sensible strategy. Unless communism was contained, Truman argued, it would sweep across Asia like a Red tide. President Eisenhower described the process another way: "You have a row of dominoes set up," he said. "You knock over the first one, and what will happen to the last one is a certainty that it will go over very quickly."

Truman provided financial aid and a few military advisers to help the French in their effort to keep communism from taking hold in Vietnam. However, by 1954, a Communist government had taken over northern Vietnam. Fearing that the Communists would gain power over all of Vietnam, Eisenhower sent 500 military advisers and spent a billion dollars in military aid. Kennedy, in turn, sent 16,000 advisers and increased financial help. "The spear point of aggression has been blunted in South Vietnam," announced Kennedy in 1963. But his statement was wrong. Rebel forces in South Vietnam, called the "Viet Cong," were trying to bring communism to South Vietnam. In 1964, they were joined by North Vietnamese army units.

Johnson's War

"I am not going to be the president who saw Southeast Asia go the way China went," Johnson promised in 1964. Three years earlier, he had visited Vietnam and returned saying that U.S. combat troops should not become involved. By 1964, however, it was clear that South Vietnam could not win the war without substantial U.S. military involvement. In that year, Johnson received the approval of Congress to "take all necessary measures" to stop armed attacks on American troops. This approval was given after Johnson described what he called an unprovoked attack by North Vietnamese torpedo boats on two American destroyers in the Gulf of Tonkin. The Congress passed, almost unanimously, the Gulf of Tonkin Resolution, which gave Johnson freedom to use armed force.

Given a blank check by Congress, Johnson rapidly increased the American military presence in Vietnam. By 1967 almost half a million U.S. troops were fighting in Vietnam. The air war over Vietnam began in 1965 with bombing in the north. Air Force bombing raids then expanded to South Vietnam and to neighboring countries where the Viet Cong were hiding and storing supplies. In 1967 the Air Force flew more than 108,000 bombing raids.

Despite heavy fire power, the conventional fighting techniques of the U.S. armed forces were no match for the unconventional **guerrilla** tactics of the Viet Cong. American B-52 bombers destroyed hundreds of supply routes and factories, leveled dozens of cities, and killed thousands of people. The Viet Cong merely moved underground, digging a 30,000-mile network of tunnels, through which they moved supplies to the south.

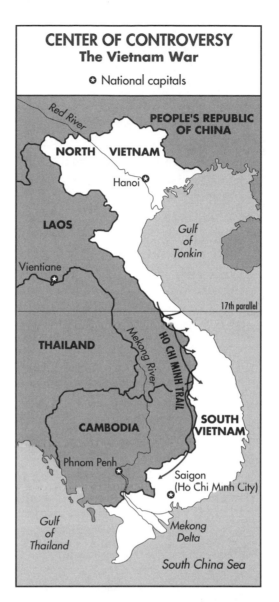

CENTER OF CONTROVERSY
The Vietnam War

✪ National capitals

Red River

PEOPLE'S REPUBLIC OF CHINA

NORTH VIETNAM

Hanoi ✪

LAOS

Gulf of Tonkin

Vientiane ✪

17th parallel

THAILAND

Mekong River

HO CHI MINH TRAIL

SOUTH VIETNAM

CAMBODIA

Phnom Penh ✪

Saigon (Ho Chi Minh City) ✪

Gulf of Thailand

Mekong Delta

South China Sea

American ground troops faced an almost impossible task, slashing their way through dense jungle, wading through muddy trails, and trekking across flooded rice paddies. The Viet Cong rarely faced U.S. troops in open battles but relied on ambushes, hit-and-run raids, booby traps, and mines. They knew the area and had the support of many villagers, even in South Vietnam. The villagers would give food to the Viet Cong and keep them informed of U.S. troop movements. In an attempt to counter the effectiveness of the Viet Cong

◀ After the Gulf of Tonkin Resolution, America's involvement in Vietnam escalated in many ways. In 1965 Operation Rolling Thunder began a massive bombing campaign above the 17th parallel—the dividing line between North and South Vietnam. The United States also heavily bombed the Ho Chi Minh Trail, the main North Vietnamese supply route that ran through Laos. Because of the stepped-up bombing and increase in the number of troops, the yearly U.S. spending on the war rose from $5.8 billion in 1965 to $28.8 billion between 1966 and 1969.

"LBJ, LBJ, how many kids have you killed today?"
—Popular marching slogan of Vietnam War protesters

As the war in Vietnam was expanding, the Students for a Democratic Society (SDS), an antiwar activist group, helped organize the first "teach-in" on March 24, 1965. It was held at the University of Michigan at Ann Arbor, only one week after the first U.S. combat troops had landed in South Vietnam.

At the teach-in, over 3,500 students and professors sang folk songs, discussed U.S. foreign policy, and debated Vietnam War issues through the night. It was the first of many teach-ins on college campuses across the country.

The largest teach-in was at the University of California at Berkeley. Twelve thousand people heard such speakers as child-care specialist Dr. Benjamin Spock, author Norman Mailer, and journalist I. F. Stone.

sympathizers, U.S troops began to burn entire villages; then they relocated the villagers to refugee camps or to cities.

The Antiwar Movement

As troop levels rose and casualty lists grew longer, opposition to the war increased. A 1965 march around the Washington Monument attracted 20,000 opponents of the war. In 1967 more than 50,000 protesters crowded onto the Pentagon steps.

Many young men refused to serve in the military during the Vietnam War because they felt that the war was unjust and unwinnable. Some burned the draft cards that indicated they were registered for military service. Thousands fled across the border to Canada to escape the draft; others were sent to jail.

By 1967 opponents of the war included Senator William Fulbright

of Arkansas, who held televised Senate hearings to examine U.S. policy in the war. Martin Luther King Jr. argued that the $2 billion the federal government was spending each month to finance the war was desperately needed to fund social programs at home. Even Americans who had once supported the war were beginning to have second thoughts. One woman expressed the sentiment of many Americans: "I want to get out, but I don't want to give up."

The Tet Offensive

In November 1967 General William Westmoreland, the commander of U.S. forces in Vietnam, announced with absolute certainty that the Viet Cong were losing the war. "We have reached an important point when the end begins to come into view," insisted the general. With these words, he helped create a dangerous myth of Ameri-

► Young men in Boston burn their draft cards to protest the Vietnam War. More than half a million men illegally avoided the draft by failing to register, changing their names, or leaving the country.

can superiority, which other spokespeople for the Johnson administration helped popularize. Then came Tet, the first day of the Vietnamese New Year, January 30, 1968. Without warning, more than 67,000 Communist forces launched a massive attack on targets throughout South Vietnam. They stormed a hundred towns and cities and a dozen U.S. military bases. They even entered the grounds of the supposedly impenetrable U.S. embassy in the capital city of Saigon, where they held out for six hours.

American and South Vietnamese forces were able to retake most of the targets within several days, but the cost was high: more than 15,000 American and South Vietnamese troops and civilians died, dozens of towns and villages lay in ruins, and more than a million South Vietnamese became refugees.

Westmoreland's myth of American supremacy had been shattered, and when the general asked for 206,000 more troops after the Tet offensive, Johnson refused. In March, Johnson announced that bombing of North Vietnam would be cut back and asked the North Vietnamese to negotiate an end to the war. He also made a startling political announcement: "I have decided that I shall not seek and I will not accept the nomination of my party for another term as your president."

The Nixon Years

In his campaign for the presidency in 1968, Richard Nixon promised an end to the unpopular war in Indochina. As president, Nixon ap-

1968: Crises and Catastrophes	
January	North Vietnamese forces launch the Tet offensive, storming more than a hundred cities and towns in South Vietnam and a dozen U.S. military bases, and entering the grounds of the American embassy in Saigon.
March	Senator Eugene McCarthy, a strong opponent of the Vietnam War, defeats President Johnson in the New Hampshire primary.
	Overwhelmed by Great Society failures and by setbacks in Vietnam, Lyndon Johnson announces his withdrawal from the 1968 presidential race.
April	Civil rights leader Martin Luther King Jr. is murdered as he stands on the balcony of the Lorraine Motel in Memphis, Tennessee. Riots follow in many cities throughout the country, including Chicago and Washington, D.C.
	More than 1,000 student antiwar and civil rights activists take over five buildings at Columbia University in New York City and occupy them for a week, until police storm the buildings and arrest the protesters.
June	While campaigning for president, Senator Robert F. Kennedy is murdered by Sirhan Sirhan, an Arab nationalist.
August	During the Democratic national convention in Chicago, a bloody confrontation between antiwar protesters and Chicago police breaks out on the city streets.
October	After finishing first and third, respectively, in the Olympic 200-meter dash, American sprinters Tommie Smith and John Carlos are ordered home from Mexico City by the U.S. Olympic Committee because they defiantly displayed the clenched-fist black power salute during the U.S. national anthem.

peared at first to keep his promise. He began to "Vietnamize" the war by slowly bringing U.S. troops home and turning the war over to the South Vietnamese. Nixon pleaded with the public to ignore the minority who were protesting the war. He appealed to what he called the great silent majority for support.

In April 1970, however, Nixon expanded the scope of the war by sending troops into Cambodia to destroy Communist bases there. A new wave of protests swept the

On November 20, 1969, 89 Native Americans took over Alcatraz island in San Francisco Bay. According to the group, an 1868 Sioux treaty entitled them to possession of unused federal lands "by right of discovery."

The group occupied for 18 months what had once been the site of Alcatraz Prison. They demanded that the government return the island to the Indians and provide money for an Indian cultural center.

The Alcatraz seizure was the first of several dramatic occupations of federal property made by Native Americans to call attention to their needs and demands. In 1972 a group of Native Americans took over the Bureau of Indian Affairs building in Washington. A year later, members of the American Indian Movement (AIM) seized 11 hostages and a trading post at Wounded Knee, South Dakota. The occupation lasted over two months, during which one Native American was killed and another was injured.

nation. Police and National Guard troops who were called in to stop peaceful demonstrations killed four students at Ohio's Kent State University and two students at Mississippi's Jackson State. Dozens were wounded in the clashes.

Week-long student demonstrations against the war erupted on college campuses across the country. In November, 300,000 antiwar protesters surrounded the Washington Monument in the nation's capital—the largest demonstration in the nation's history. The opposition only increased when the *New York Times* published the secret "Pentagon Papers," giving evidence that the Johnson administration had lied about U.S. involvement in the war.

The morale of American troops in Vietnam fell to an all-time low. The daily horrors of fighting an unwinnable war became too much for many soldiers to bear. Discipline problems became common; some

soldiers turned to drugs and alcohol to escape. In the United States, a group of disenchanted veterans formed Vietnam Veterans Against the War.

All the while, Nixon continued to pull troops out of Vietnam. By 1972, fewer than 25,000 American soldiers remained in Vietnam. At the same time, Henry Kissinger, Nixon's national security adviser, was holding secret negotiations with the North Vietnamese in Paris. When the talks stalled in December 1972, Nixon ordered what became known as the "Christmas bombings." For 12 days, American bombers pounded major cities in North Vietnam—the most massive bombing of the war. Thousands of civilians died.

By the end of January, the North Vietnamese had returned to the bargaining table and agreed to a cease-fire. Not long after American troops left South Vietnam in March, however, fighting broke out

▶ To control rising student unrest at Kent State University after the American invasion of Cambodia, Ohio governor James Rhodes dispatched the National Guard to the campus. On May 4, 1970, the guard was ordered to break up an antiwar rally. After the crowd refused to disperse, some of the soldiers opened fire without warning. Four students were killed, and ten more were injured. The Kent State tragedy became a symbol of the needless bloodshed associated with Vietnam.

once again. Two years later, Americans watched on television as Communist troops marched into Saigon. The city surrendered on April 30, 1975, and the nation of South Vietnam soon followed. Vietnam was reunited under the government of the Communist North.

The United States, a wealthy and technologically advanced nation, had lost a major war against a determined band of **Third World** guerrillas. Nixon had promised "peace with honor"; instead, the nation suffered defeat.

THE CIVIL RIGHTS MOVEMENT

In June 1964 Andrew Goodman, Michael Schwerner, and James Chaney drove into the small town of Philadelphia, Mississippi. These civil rights workers—two white and one black—had come to investigate two racial incidents in nearby Neshoba County. They had received reports that members of the Ku Klux Klan (KKK) had beaten three black men and set fire to the Mt. Zion Church, where a "freedom school" for black voters was being organized.

In Philadelphia, the deputy sheriff arrested the three on a charge of speeding and suspicion of burning the church themselves. The men were jailed for six hours, fined $20 each, and then released at 10 P.M. They drove off into the night and were not seen again alive. Several days later, their bodies were found buried underneath

an earthen dam. Evidence provided to the FBI by an informant confirmed that the brutal murders were the work of members of the KKK chapter in Mississippi.

The Civil Rights Act of 1964

In the midst of the widespread furor over these killings, President Johnson was preparing to sign the Civil Rights Act of 1964. The bill had actually been sent to Congress by President Kennedy in 1963. "We are confronted primarily with a moral issue," Kennedy had explained. "It is as old as the scriptures and is as clear as the American Constitution." With those words, Kennedy followed a trail blazed by Dr. Martin Luther King Jr., who spoke of his "dream that one day this nation will rise and live out the true meaning of its creed: 'We hold these truths to be self-evident; that all men are created equal.'"

After some initial resistance by southern Democrats, both the

▲ Americans and other foreigners were quickly evacuated from downtown Saigon as it was on the verge of falling to the North Vietnamese in May 1975. Many South Vietnamese also tried desperately to flee on the airlifts.

▲ Before a crowd of 200,000 gathered at the Lincoln Memorial in Washington in 1963, Martin Luther King Jr.'s compelling "I Have a Dream" speech set the tone for the era. He challenged America to fulfill the promises of the Declaration of Independence and Constitution for all its people. King continued his nonviolent crusade until he was assassinated in 1968 outside his Memphis motel room by James Earl Ray.

House and the Senate passed the Civil Rights bill. "No army can withstand the strength of an idea whose time has come," explained a Senate leader. Johnson signed the bill into law on July 2, 1964.

The Civil Rights Act of 1964 was the most comprehensive civil rights legislation enacted up to that time. All hotels, motels, restaurants, lunch counters, theaters, sports arenas, and other businesses that catered to the public had to serve everyone, regardless of color. Most businesses in southern cities and large towns took immediate action to integrate. Through the act, though, responsi-

bility for enforcing desegregation shifted from the states to the federal government.

Selma and the Right to Vote

Also in 1964, the Twenty-fourth Amendment to the Constitution was ratified. It made unconstitutional the practice in some southern states of charging a **poll tax** to vote in federal elections—a practice meant to keep blacks from voting. Neither the Civil Rights Act nor the Twenty-fourth Amendment, however, ensured black Americans full access to the voting booth. Many southern states required black citizens to pass difficult literacy tests before they could register to vote. Most failed the tests, which were designed to keep blacks from registering. In the city of Selma, Alabama, for example, half the citizens were black, but 99 percent of voters were white. King and other civil rights leaders decided to force the government to correct this injustice in Selma and elsewhere.

On March 7, 1965, 600 civil rights demonstrators began a protest march from Selma to Montgomery, the state capital, ignoring Governor George Wallace's ban on the demonstration. As the marchers reached the Edmund Pettus Bridge outside Selma, state troopers gave them two minutes to disperse, then waded into the crowd firing tear gas and swinging clubs. Television news film showed graphic scenes of defenseless men and women being bludgeoned to the ground. Enraged northerners called upon the president to take action.

Johnson immediately dispatched federal troops to line the route of the march, which proceeded peacefully on March 21. He also promised to send a bill to Congress that would extend to blacks in the South the right to vote. The bill became the Voting Rights Act of 1965. The act stated that literacy tests could be used only in areas where more than 50 percent of voting-age citizens had actually voted in 1964. Within the next three years, more than 740,000 new black voters were added to the rolls. They voted, too: hundreds of new black officials won election to offices across the South.

A Movement Divided

One summer day in June 1966, two key leaders of the civil rights movement marched arm in arm down U.S. Highway 51 in Mississippi: Dr. Martin Luther King Jr. and Stokely Carmichael of the Student Nonviolent Coordinating Committee (SNCC). They were completing a 220-mile protest march started by James Meredith, a young black man who had been gunned down while demonstrating his right to travel without fear in Mississippi. King and Carmichael stopped at town squares along the way, speaking to the crowds. When they finished, King and his supporters began to sing their theme song, "We Shall Overcome." Carmichael and his militant followers sang too, but they used different words: "We Shall Overrun."

That march, begun in unity, showed the deep disagreement among civil rights leaders about strategy. King continued to advo-

cate nonviolent protest; other black leaders became impatient. Some began to move toward black separatism. Elijah Muhammad, a leader of the Nation of Islam, commonly known as the "Black Muslims," had been one of the first. "Negroes must take over for themselves lands, property, and civilization," he insisted. "Get away from the white man. . . . Stand up and fight. Do the same by them as they do by you."

Malcolm X was also a Black Muslim. Though he had left the Nation of Islam in a leadership struggle, he took up the cry until his assassination in 1965. "The

Thurgood Marshall: Defender of Civil Rights

Throughout his legal career, Thurgood Marshall (shown here with his wife Vivian) was a leading proponent of American civil rights reform. After receiving a law degree from Howard University, Marshall offered his legal skills to the Baltimore branch of the National Association for the Advancement of Colored People (NAACP). In 1940 he became the head of the NAACP's Legal Defense and Education Fund.

During the 1940s and 1950s, Marshall argued 32 civil rights cases before the Supreme Court and wrote briefs for 11 others brought to the Court. Among these was the 1954 *Brown v. Board of Education of Topeka, Kansas*, in which the Supreme Court decided that segregated school systems denied minority children an equal education.

Because of Marshall's reputation for engineering important changes in civil rights laws, President Kennedy appointed him to the U.S. Court of Appeals in 1961. He became U.S. solicitor general in 1965 under President Johnson; in this position he represented the U.S. government before the Supreme Court. In 1967 Johnson nominated Marshall to become an associate justice of the U.S. Supreme Court. When he was confirmed by the Senate later that year, Marshall became the first black member of the High Court. He retired from the bench in 1991.

day of nonviolent resistance is over," he proclaimed in one of his brilliant and fiery speeches. "It was stones yesterday, Molotov cocktails today; it will be hand grenades tomorrow and whatever else is available the next day."

Stokely Carmichael believed in black political action, which he called "black power." As head of the SNCC, Carmichael helped form a black political party in Lowndes County, Alabama. The symbol of the Lowndes County Freedom Organization was a black panther about to spring. According to Carmichael, black power meant saying to politicians, "Look, buddy, we're not laying a vote on you unless you lay so many schools, hospitals, playgrounds and jobs on us."

Black Rage

Despite new civil rights laws, black Americans, especially those living in large northern cities, became increasingly frustrated. The civil rights movement focused on problems in the South. Meanwhile, northern blacks felt ignored, even though their rights were also being violated. In addition, blacks resented Johnson's willingness to spend billions of dollars on the Vietnam War instead of continuing the War on Poverty. It was, in Malcolm X's words, "a powder keg situation."

On August 11, 1965, police in the Los Angeles neighborhood of Watts stopped a young black man for a traffic violation. They beat him. When a pregnant woman nearby protested, they clubbed her down, too. Watts exploded into an angry riot. In six long and terrible days of fighting and looting, 34 people died, more than 1,000 were injured, and the police made 4,000 arrests. More than 1,000 buildings were damaged or destroyed, with a

Black Is Beautiful

It is time to stop being ashamed of being black—time to stop trying to be white. When you see your daughter playing in the field, with her nappy hair, her wide nose and her thick lips, tell her she is beautiful. Tell your daughter she is beautiful.

This plea by SNCC chairman Stokely Carmichael illustrates the dramatic social revolution that transformed black life in the 1960s. The "Black Pride" movement gave black Americans a new image and a new self-respect. "Say it loud—I'm black and I'm proud," shouted soul singer James Brown.

For very many black Americans, black pride meant finding their ethnic identity in the culture of historic and modern-day Africa. African clothing and jewelry and Afro hairstyles became popular. Works of art by African painters and sculptors decorated the homes of countless black people. Many blacks began to call themselves "Afro-Americans"; some

even returned to African religions.

Black pride manifested itself on the nation's college and university campuses through black students' demands for black studies courses and the establishment of black studies departments. These courses were designed to focus on black history and culture, which had been ignored in history textbooks up to that time. Throughout the country,

▼ ▼ ▼

"We are not fighting for integration, nor are we fighting for separation. We are fighting for recognition as human beings. We are fighting for . . . human rights."

—Malcolm X in a speech in New York, 1964

blacks began to demand the right to have a voice in decisions in their communities. They wanted to be heard on economic, educational, and political issues that affected their lives.

property loss of almost $40 million. Two years later, a routine raid on a black speakeasy (unlicensed bar) in Detroit turned into the worst race riot of the decade.

Between 1964 and 1967, 58 cities across the nation felt the full fury of black rage. Minor incidents between police and black citizens mushroomed into battles. President Johnson appointed a commission to study the problem. Its findings, called the "Kerner Report," concluded that "the nation is rapidly moving toward two increasingly separate Americas."

The Kerner Report recommended several steps to integrate American society, but the violence did not stop. When Martin Luther King Jr. was assassinated on April 4, 1968, an outburst of black violence swept once more through black communities across the nation. "We've got some difficult days ahead," King predicted the night before he died. "But I want you to know tonight . . . that we as a people will get to the promised land!"

The Post-King Years

Not since the post–Civil War era had so many gains in civil rights been made so quickly. In large measure, the success of the movement came from the inspiring leadership of Dr. King. His power to persuade and his deep-felt sense of moral

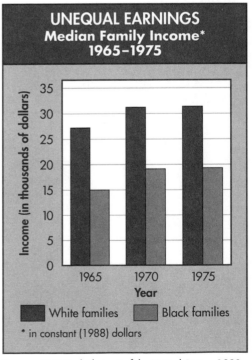

UNEQUAL EARNINGS
Median Family Income*
1965–1975

Income (in thousands of dollars)

35
30
25
20
15
10
5
0

1965   1970   1975
Year

■ White families   ■ Black families

* in constant (1988) dollars

Source: *Statistical Abstract of the United States, 1990.*

◀ In spite of civil rights gains, the income gap between black and white families remained high. The leveling off of both groups reflected the economic problems of the early 1970s, which signaled the end of the post–World War II boom.

purpose gained him the respect of blacks and whites. After his death, the movement focused on the hard work of changing the foundations of a segregated society.

RICHARD NIXON'S POLITICAL CAREER

Richard M. Nixon, whatever his shortcomings, was an extremely astute politician. That became clear early in his career. Using the growing fear of communism as a weapon to discredit his opponent, the California Republican won election to the U.S. House of Representatives in 1946. As a member of the House Committee on Un-American Activities, Congressman Nixon became known nationally during the committee's investigation of the activities of Alger Hiss. Hiss, a former high-level State Department official, was accused of carrying on espionage for the USSR during the 1930s.

After two terms in the House, Nixon was elected to the Senate in 1950, again by suggesting his opponent had dangerous left-wing tendencies. Two years later, Dwight Eisenhower chose Nixon, by then one of the bright young stars of the Republican party, to be his vice presidential running mate. Then political disaster threatened. Stories began to circulate about a secret fund of political contributions that Nixon used to support a lavish lifestyle. Quickly, Nixon went on the offensive. The fund had been used only for travel between Washington and California, he told a nationwide television audience. He did admit to receiving a cocker spaniel named Checkers as a gift. But his young daughters loved Checkers, and he was not going to give up the dog. Many Americans loved Nixon's speech, and Eisenhower and Nixon won by a huge margin.

Nixon proved a capable vice president. He traveled widely, and his reputation was dramatically enhanced by his famous "kitchen debate" on democracy with Soviet premier Nikita Khrushchev. When Nixon ran as the Republican candidate for president against Kennedy in 1960, however, he lost. Nixon performed poorly during a series of televised debates with Kennedy, whose humor and charm captivated American audiences. Kennedy's margin of victory was very narrow, however. He received

▼ Although Nixon's margin of victory in the popular vote was very slim—he won 43.4 percent to Humphrey's 42.9 percent—the GOP ticket swept through many states in the West, Midwest, and South to win a solid majority of electoral votes.

A REPUBLICAN VICTORY
The Presidential Election of 1968

Republican:
Richard M. Nixon, **302**

Democratic:
Hubert H. Humphrey, **191**

American Independent:
George Wallace, **45**

10 Electoral votes

only 100,000 more popular votes than Nixon. The electoral vote was close also—303 to 219.

The 1968 Campaign

The 1968 presidential election offered Republicans an opportunity. The war in Vietnam had completely undone the Democratic presidency of Lyndon Johnson. Violence was rampant in America's cities, and college campuses seethed with protest. The **counterculture** seemed determined to destroy the nation's traditional values. When the Democrats met in Chicago to choose a candidate for president, the party was still reeling from the effects of the assassination of Robert Kennedy, one of those campaigning for the candidacy. Vice President Hubert Humphrey, whom the convention delegates chose as the Democratic candidate, was closely tied to the policies of Johnson's administration. When antiwar protesters gathered outside the Democratic convention to protest Humphrey's nomination, the result was a bloody confrontation with Chicago police.

Nixon returned to national politics to capture the 1968 Republican nomination. Sensing what the majority of Americans wanted, he promised law and order in America, a quick end to costly Great Society programs, and peace with honor in Vietnam. The nation responded to Nixon's agenda for stability and a return to traditional values, and he won the election.

President Nixon

"We want to bring America together," Nixon claimed in his victory speech. In fact, the new

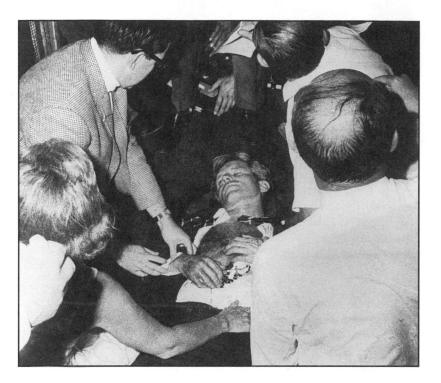

▲ Five years after his brother was killed, Senator Robert Kennedy was murdered in Los Angeles in June 1968. He had just given a victory speech after the California primary. His assassin, Arab immigrant Sirhan Sirhan, apparently objected to Kennedy's support of Israel.

conservatism of the Nixon administration had the opposite effect. Nixon believed the liberal policies of the 1960s had neglected the needs of the "silent majority" of Americans—"the forgotten Americans, the non-shouters, the non-demonstrators." He was determined to shift government policies to benefit the middle class.

Of course, several formidable forces stood in Nixon's way: a powerful civil rights movement, strong antiwar sentiment, growing concern for the environment, and a Democrat-controlled Congress. At times, he had to compromise. Nixon approved bills to establish the Environmental Protection Agency and the Occupational Safety and Health Administration. He also signed laws to fund low-cost housing and boost Social Security benefits.

Nevertheless, under Nixon's persistent leadership, the nation began to steer a more conservative

"Let us begin by committing ourselves to the truth, to see it like it is and tell it like it is, to find the truth, to speak the truth and to live the truth. That's what we will do."

—Richard M. Nixon in his presidential nomination acceptance speech in Miami, August 8, 1968

course. One key set of programs, which he called the "New Federalism," tried to cut funding for many Great Society initiatives and shift responsibility for antipoverty welfare programs back to the states. To combat violence and unrest, John Mitchell, Nixon's attorney general, gave the police broad new powers to collect evidence and detain suspects. Nixon and Mitchell also used federal agencies, such as the FBI and the Internal Revenue Service (IRS), to harass their liberal opponents and spy on civil rights groups.

To gain support among white conservatives in the South, Nixon began to attack the civil rights movement. He blocked court-ordered integration of schools in South Carolina and Mississippi, and he opposed the extension of the Voting Rights Act of 1965. Nixon also appointed four conservative justices to fill vacancies on the Supreme Court.

A New Foreign Policy

Despite his failure in Vietnam, Nixon made dramatic diplomatic advances in other parts of the world. Henry Kissinger, a skilled and clever negotiator, served first as Nixon's national security adviser and then as his secretary of state. Kissinger and the president saw that economic power was replacing military might as the key source of international power. As a result, they rejected the Cold War policy of confrontation between the two military superpowers, the United States and the Soviet Union. Instead they pursued a new policy called **détente,** which means a lessening of tensions. Under détente, the United States would seek to improve relations with the Soviet Union and negotiate arms reductions.

Nixon and Kissinger advocated a **balance of power** among the world's five economic superpowers: the United States, the USSR,

▶ President Nixon tours the Great Wall with Chinese leaders in February 1972. His historic trip to China signaled a new era in Cold War international relations. Nixon and Chinese premier Jou En-lai (Chou En-lai) discussed Taiwan, Vietnam, and their mutual distrust of the Soviet Union.

Japan, China, and the European Economic Community. Economic cooperation among nations would make the world a safer and better place, the president said. Nixon, the once-strident anticommunist, stunned the world by making trips in 1972 to both China and Russia, the main Communist powers.

Nixon's well-publicized visits abroad and Kissinger's assurance that "peace is at hand" in Vietnam helped Nixon overpower George McGovern and a still deeply divided Democratic party in the 1972 presidential election. Nixon won by a landslide, by the widest margin in U.S. history.

NIXON UNDONE: THE WATERGATE SCANDAL

Richard Nixon's landslide victory in 1972 did not wipe out the dark side of his administration. "King Richard," as some critics called him, often acted as if the nation were his personal kingdom. On his own, Nixon froze funds for federal programs he disliked and ordered U.S. troops to invade Cambodia. By law, both these actions required congressional approval. Nixon wielded his "imperial" power through an inner circle of loyal and trusted aides, including chief of staff H. R. Haldeman and chief domestic adviser John Ehrlichman.

In 1971 Nixon directed Charles Colson, his special counsel, to draw up a secret list of the administration's enemies. Colson listed 200 individuals and 18 organizations, including prominent liberal politicians, black leaders, journalists, and even movie stars. Then Nixon ordered the FBI to spy on his enemies and discredit them. "You were either for us or against us, and if you were against us we were against you," recalled one Nixon aide. The president also approved an illegal plan to combat the antiwar movement by spying on the activities of antiwar groups.

▼ Three of Nixon's top aides, H. R. Haldeman, John Dean, and John Ehrlichman (left to right), became household names during the Senate Watergate hearings. Dean, Nixon's former counsel, implicated his two colleagues and the president in the plot to cover up the Watergate affair. Though Haldeman and Ehrlichman denied this to the Senate, they were later found guilty in court.

▼ North Carolina senator Sam Ervin ran the televised hearings of the Senate Watergate committee. His down-home wit and wisdom made him a national folk hero.

The Watergate Break-in

As fiction, the Watergate scandal would be a thrilling tale of political intrigue. But the truth is a chronicle of Nixon's growing hunger for power. To raise money for his 1972 reelection campaign, Nixon asked John Mitchell to resign as attorney general and set up the Committee to Re-elect the President, known as "CREEP." Mitchell raised more than $60 million, much of it illegally. To make certain no one heard about these activities, Mitchell formed a secret unit of investigators, nicknamed "plumbers," to stop security leaks within the Nixon administration.

One of the plumbers proposed a daring plan to Mitchell: to break into the headquarters of the Democratic party, copy their campaign plans, and wiretap their phones. The plan was approved by Mitchell and put into action on June 17, 1972. One major hitch developed: the burglars were caught in the act by an alert security guard at the Watergate complex in Washington, D.C. At the scene of the arrest, police found an address book containing the name Howard Hunt (a

CREEP employee). Beside it was a telephone number and a brief note: "W. House."

By mid-October, months of persistent investigation had given *Washington Post* reporters Bob Woodward and Carl Bernstein enough information to write a sensational series of stories linking the break-in to CREEP and the White House. Nixon officials exploded with fury, calling the article "a senseless pack of lies." Rumors began to circulate, but nothing definite could be established linking the burglars and CREEP prior to the November election. Early in 1973, however, one burglar agreed to cooperate with the grand jury investigation in exchange for a light sentence. The true story of CREEP's crimes and the cover-up by White House officials began to come to light. The Nixon administration was unraveling.

Nixon denied any knowledge of or participation in the cover-up. During televised Senate hearings into the Watergate affair in the summer of 1973, White House officials testified to many illegal actions by the White House, including the Watergate break-in and its cover-up. More than 50 administration officials faced criminal charges. Most damaging to Nixon was the discovery of his secret White House tape recordings. Claiming to be protecting national security, he would not turn over the tapes until April 1974—and those were edited. Two events in July 1974 led to Nixon's downfall. The Supreme Court ordered Nixon to release the unedited tapes, and the House Judiciary Committee voted to impeach, or indict, the

◀ With his daughter Tricia looking on, an anguished president tells his staff of his decision to resign.

president. When Nixon released the unedited tapes in early August, they proved his involvement in the cover-up.

Nixon announced his resignation of the presidency on television on August 8, 1974. He was the first president in history to resign. The once-proud president, who had insisted in 1973, "I am not a crook," left the nation's highest elected office in humiliation.

Gerald Ford and the Return to Normalcy

"Our long national nightmare is over," promised the new president, Gerald Ford. After serving 25 years as a representative from Michigan, Ford had been appointed vice president by Nixon when Spiro Agnew resigned because of corruption charges. "I have not sought this enormous responsibility, but I will not shirk it," Ford declared. He became the only U.S. president never to have been elected as either president or vice president.

In an attempt to leave the Watergate scandal behind, Ford pardoned Nixon for any crimes he might have committed. He then turned to address the nation's economic crisis. Productivity was plummeting, and prices were soaring, a disaster brought on mainly by an Arab oil **embargo** and the resulting energy crisis. Ford's remedy was a plan called "WIN: Whip Inflation Now," but it failed to avert the recession of 1974–1975, which became the worst economic slowdown since the Great Depression. Although most Americans liked Ford personally, many disliked his handling of economic issues and foreign policy. His pardon of Nixon was also widely unpopular. In the 1976 presidential election, the nation turned to Jimmy Carter, a Democrat and former governor of Georgia.

THE CREDIBILITY GAP

A national opinion poll in 1975 found that 69 percent of all Americans believed that "over the last 10 years, this country's leaders have consistently lied to the people." In addition, public confidence in physicians dropped from 73 percent in 1966 to 42 percent in 1975. Confidence in big business dipped from 55 percent to 16 percent during the same time period.

▼ The campaign for women's liberation took to the streets in the late sixties.

THE WOMEN'S MOVEMENT

The women's movement was touched off by the 1963 publication of Betty Friedan's *The Feminine Mystique.* "If I am right," wrote Friedan, "the problem that has no name stirring in the minds of so many American women today is not a matter of loss of femininity or too much education, or the demands of domesticity. . . . We can no longer ignore the voice within women that says: 'I want something more than my husband and my children and my home.'" Women who had worked in the civil rights movement began to feel that they, like the black Americans they were demonstrating for, were being treated as second-class citizens.

The problem may have had no name at first, but women knew precisely what they wanted: equality. The 1963 report of the President's Commission on the Status of Women painted a grim picture.

Women made up one-third of the labor force, but most held low-paying jobs; only 5 percent of all managers and administrators were women. Besides, for every dollar men earned, women with the same jobs were paid only 59 cents. Women held only 5 percent of all state legislative seats in the nation, and only 13 seats in Congress. While the birth control pill had given women a new level of sexual freedom, many feminists believed women should have the freedom to choose to have an abortion as well.

Most feminists agreed that the key to women's liberation was concerted political action. The Equal Pay Act of 1963 forced employers to pay women the same as men for doing the same job, and the Civil Rights Act of 1964 outlawed job **discrimination** on the basis of sex. Yet women knew these laws alone would not bring equality.

NOW

In 1966 Betty Friedan and other activists formed a civil rights organization for women, the National Organization for Women (NOW). Through NOW, women sought the passage of an equal rights amendment (see feature), better child care, maternity benefits, equal job-training opportunities, and abortion rights. By 1974 NOW membership had grown to 40,000 people in 1,000 chapters across the nation.

NOW's political strength compelled the nation to take seriously the question of women's equality. Even so, some men still thought the movement was a struggle over trivial issues, such as whether a man should hold a door open for

a woman or whether a woman should pay for a meal when a man and woman went out on a date.

The concrete legislative gains achieved by NOW and other activists were anything but trivial, however. In 1970 the U.S. Labor Department required all companies with federal contracts to employ a certain percentage of women. The Education Act of 1972 outlawed sex discrimination in education—all classes, including shop and cooking classes, would be open to all students. This law also required schools to provide females with equal opportunity in athletic programs. By 1976 women could attend the military academies at West Point and Annapolis. Perhaps the most dramatic symbol of women's new freedom came in 1973. In its *Roe v. Wade* decision, the Supreme Court ruled that women have a constitutional right to choose an abortion during the early months of pregnancy.

The success of NOW led to the founding of the National Women's Political Caucus by journalist Gloria Steinem (founder of *Ms.* magazine) and others in 1971. The Women's Campaign Fund began in 1974. These organizations worked for the election of women to political office. As a result of their efforts, Ella Grasso was elected governor of Connecticut in 1974, the first woman governor who was not her husband's successor. In the same year, Janet Gray Hayes won election as mayor of San Jose, California, the first woman mayor of a [major] [Am]erican city. By 1976 [they we]re on the way to getting [what the]y wanted. But there was [still] a long road to travel.

The ERA: Equal Rights Amendment

"Equality of rights under the law shall not be abridged by the United States or by any state on account of sex." That sentence and two other brief clauses almost became the Twenty-seventh Amendment to the U.S. Constitution. But it did not, and the reason is worth telling.

▼ ▼ ▼

"Equality of rights under the law shall not be abridged by the United States or by any state on account of sex."

—Equal Rights Amendment

The Equal Rights Amendment, or ERA, was first introduced in Congress by the National Woman's Party in 1923. It was put before Congress every year after that for many decades, but it never became law. Women's groups opposed the ERA, since many women's rights were already protected by other laws.

During the 1960s, however, judges began to strike down these protective laws because they were in conflict with the Civil Rights Act of 1964. The League of Women Voters and NOW sprang into action and put their political power behind the ERA. It was easily passed by the House in 1970 and by the Senate in 1972. The amendment then had seven years in which to be ratified, or approved, by three-fourths of the states.

Thirty-one states ratified the ERA in 1973, and then it stalled. Congress extended the ratification period until 1982, but that did not help. Only 35 states approved it—three short of the necessary 38.

Why did the ERA fail? Feminist leaders seriously underestimated the power of conservative women's groups, who rallied to prevent what they saw as an endangerment to traditional family values. STOP ERA, an organization formed by Phyllis Schlafly in 1972, led the vigorous opposition campaign. It made the exaggerated claims that the ERA would send women into combat, destroy the family, require the government to fund abortions, and force men and women to use the same public restrooms. The stir that STOP ERA aroused, however, quickly and permanently halted the amendment's momentum.

THE COUNTERCULTURE

Most teenagers in the 1950s seemed basically content with the world they inherited from their parents. They generally accepted its traditional values and took their place in its social order without protest. The youth of the 1960s, in contrast, believed adults had made a mess of things. They saw the Vietnam War raging, the earth being polluted, civil rights being violated, and America's cities burning. The values of the established generation—conformity, hard work, consumerism—had failed.

The new generation created a radically different culture, based on new values. Instead of working for the future, they immersed themselves in the present, adopting the "anything goes" philosophy of the 1950s Beatnik movement: "Do your own thing, and do it *now!*" Jerry Rubin, a leader of the sixties counterculture, looked back on the movement many years later, describing the era of his youth this way: "The rock bands created a tribal, animal energy. We were a religion, a family, a culture, with our own music, our own dress, our own human relationships, our own stimulants, our own media. And we believed that our energy would turn on the world."

Rubin was right: it was a full-fledged culture. The "hippies," as the rebellious youth came to be called, flocked to the East Village in New York City and Haight-Ashbury in San Francisco, both centers of the counterculture movement. They shocked adults with their long hair and ragged clothing. Torn blue jeans, beaded headbands, fringed jackets, tie-dyed shirts, psychedelic colors, and bare feet or sandals became the new dress code. "Make America Beautiful—give a hippie a haircut" became a popular slogan among older adults.

▶ The sixties counterculture rejected traditional institutions in favor of new arrangements based on love and freedom. Hippies wanted to free themselves from the patterns, habits, labels, and possessions of the older generation. They gathered for "be-ins" and "love-ins," where they could "go with the flow" of a shared experience.

The New Generation

The counterculture also had a new agenda. Their search for intense and meaningful experiences led hippies to explore new ways of living. Young people in the 1960s shared their living space with anyone and everyone. In cities across the nation, hippies would "crash" for a night or two at someone's "pad," sleeping on a spare mattress tossed onto the floor. Some hippies retreated to rural areas to create their own **utopian communities,** where all were equal and free. The Hog Farm, Soul Experience, and Drop City, U.S.A., were three of the many experimental communities. Many of these attempts to create a new social structure were short-lived.

The new generation's idea of total freedom and personal absorption extended to sex. The key to sexual freedom was the widespread availability of birth control pills. Both men and women enthusiastically heeded the call to "make love, not war." They suffered from it too: sexually transmitted diseases climbed at an alarming rate.

Drugs were perhaps the most obvious route to the sensual ecstasy sought by the new generation. Timothy Leary, a onetime Harvard University professor, became the high priest of the drug culture. While other hippies sought spiritual uplift through astrology or magic, Leary presented a new religion of love and freedom, accessible through the **hallucinatory drug** LSD. "LSD is Western yoga," claimed Leary. "The aim of all Eastern religion, like the aim of LSD, is basically to get high; that is, to expand your consciousness

Psychologist Timothy Leary, leader of the LSD movement, told his followers to "tune in, turn on, drop out." His message on the liberating power of hallucinatory drugs eventually became discredited by the growing problems of drug overdose and addiction.

and find ecstasy and revelation within."

Throughout the sixties, young people gathered for "love-ins" and "be-ins." For example, 400,000 gathered at Bethel, New York, in 1969, for the Woodstock festival— "three days of peace and music." They listened to rock music, wore radical new clothing or no clothes at all, drank beer, smoked marijuana, and made love. Woodstock was noteworthy because it was a peaceful celebration of the music and lifestyle of the youth of the 1960s.

Distrust of the older generation was common. "Don't trust anyone over 30" and "Question Authority!" were often-repeated slogans of the movement. More than anything, however, the youth of the 1960s were drawn together by their opposition to the Vietnam War and support of civil rights. Although the counterculture had an impact on American food, fashion, music, and art, its most telling slogan was also its most profound contribution to the agenda of the 1960s: "Peace."

NEW WORDS
Afro (hairstyle)
credibility gap
gross out
nerd
sexism
workaholic
zip code

THE WORLD

The social and political unrest experienced in the United States in the sixties and early seventies was felt elsewhere in the world as well. As in America, much of the anger was voiced by youth who were unhappy with the values and methods of their parents' generation—the "establishment."

On the world stage, America represented the establishment. Its offenses loomed large, with the Vietnam War at the center. The anti-American sentiment during the sixties stemmed partly from the sense that since World War II the United Sates had been calling too many of the shots in world affairs, making too many decisions on behalf of others. And especially in Europe, many felt that the Cold War and the arms race it created made no sense.

But new economic strength was turning once weak nations into powers during this era. West Germany and Japan particularly

AT A GLANCE

- ► Tension in the Middle East
- ► The Western Hemisphere
- ► Western Europe Grows Stronger
- ► The Soviet Union's Heavy Hand
- ► China Opens Up
- ► Growth, Strife, and Suffering in Asia
- ► Revolution and Independence in Africa

emerged as major forces no longer under America's shadow. In the Middle East, the Arab nations drew together to convert the economic might of oil production into political power. Their oil embargo of 1973 delivered a blow to Western economies dependent on imported oil. The Arab countries fared less well, however, in their ongoing struggle with Israel, one of the many regional conflicts of the period.

In the early seventies, two significant changes shifted the delicate balance between the two superpowers, the United States and the USSR. First, a series of agreements eased tensions between the two countries. Second, the United States opened diplomatic relations with China, the world's most populous nation and second most powerful Communist country. This shift in the balance of power signified a new acceptance of political differences and hope for world peace.

DATAFILE

World Population	1965	1975
Total	3.3 bil.	4.1 bil.
Africa	318 mil.	415 mil.
Asia	1.9 bil.	2.4 bil.
Australia and Oceania	17 mil.	21 mil.
Central and South America	250 mil.	322 mil.
Europe (not including USSR)	445 mil.	474 mil.
North America	214 mil.	239 mil.
USSR	231 mil.	255 mil.

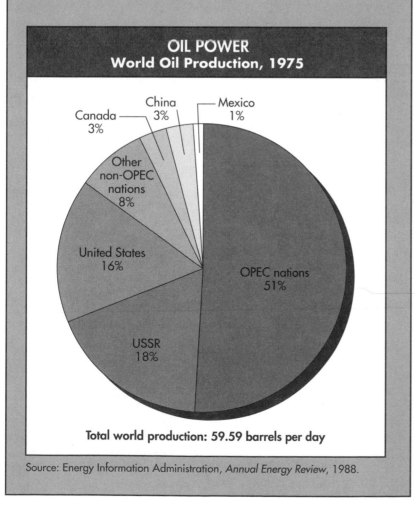

OIL POWER
World Oil Production, 1975

China 3%
Mexico 1%
Canada 3%
Other non-OPEC nations 8%
United States 16%
OPEC nations 51%
USSR 18%

Total world production: 59.59 barrels per day

Source: Energy Information Administration, *Annual Energy Review*, 1988.

TENSION IN THE MIDDLE EAST

On the eastern shore of the Mediterranean Sea lies a narrow strip of land less than 150 miles long. Since ancient times, the land had been called Palestine. To three of the world's major religions—Judaism, Islam, and Christianity—it is the Holy Land. Many of the world's Arabs and Jews also consider it their homeland, and therein lies the problem. In 1948 the Jewish state of Israel was established in Palestine. A group of Arab nations immediately tried to destroy Israel, but the Arab armies were soundly defeated by determined Jewish settlers. War erupted in the region once again in 1956, when Israel, Britain, and France stopped an attempt by Gamal Abdel Nasser, leader of Egypt, to take over the Suez Canal.

Between 1948 and 1967, Israel flourished. Its population quadrupled, farm output jumped from $15 million to $480 million, and the **gross national product** (GNP) grew 12.7 percent a year, the fourth highest rate in the world. Israel's deep-rooted conflict with its Arab neighbors, however, continued to simmer.

The Six-Day War

By the spring of 1967, tensions in the region heated almost to the boiling point. Small-scale battles constantly threatened to erupt into major conflict. When Egypt blockaded Israel's only access to the Red Sea, war seemed almost certain. Even though U.S. government

The Palestinians

▲ Representing the Palestinian people, PLO chief Yasser Arafat urged the United Nations in 1974 to create a Palestinian state in which "Arabs, Jews, and Christians could live in peace."

The expansion of Israel created a huge problem in the Middle East: the displacement of millions of Arabs who called Palestine their home. These Palestinians were united by a burning desire to take back the land that once was theirs.

In 1964 the Arab League formed the Palestine Liberation Organization (PLO), which became an alliance of **guerrilla** forces dedicated to the destruction of Israel. One of the most powerful and best-organized of these forces was Al Fatah, led by Yasser Arafat. In 1969 Arafat was chosen to lead the PLO, which the UN recognized as "the representative of the Palestinian people" in 1974. *Our Palestine,* the magazine of Al Fatah, called on Arabs to make the world listen:

> Sons of the Catastrophe, you cannot forget . . . the loss of lands and honor. Our destiny is being shaped, but our voice is not heard. . . . We tell you that our voice, the voice of the Palestinian people, will not be heard until the sons of Palestine stand together in one rank. . . . Then you will find the world attentive to your merest whisper . . . yes, just a whisper.

The voice of the PLO was the voice of terror as well as of protest. The Al Fatah group specialized in guerrilla raids on targets in Israel, while another arm of the PLO hijacked international airliners and held the passengers hostage. These terrorist tactics worsened the already explosive atmosphere in the Middle East.

intelligence analysts from the CIA predicted a quick Israeli victory, Israel faced overwhelming odds. The Syrian and Jordanian armies were ready to the east, and the powerful Egyptian army had taken a position in the Sinai Peninsula to the west. All were equipped with modern Soviet jets, tanks, and other weapons.

Furthermore, Egypt and Syria had forged an Arab alliance against Israel. Nasser boldly declared, "If Israel begins any aggression against Egypt or Syria, the battle against Israel will be total and its object will be the destruction of Israel." Iraq and other Arab nations soon joined the alliance.

Israeli military commanders had only one hope of defeating their Arab opponents: strike first and strike hard. In the early hours of June 5, 1967, 300 low-flying Israeli fighter-bombers launched precision attacks against airfields in Egypt, Jordan, Syria, and Iraq. By nightfall, some 400 Arab planes had been crippled, and Israel controlled the skies. Even so, Syrian radio promised, "We will destroy Israel in four days."

Meanwhile, 235,000 Israeli ground troops were swiftly organized for battle. Eight hundred tanks and 30,000 men swept west into the desert and smashed through Nasser's border forces. Within three days, these Israeli troops had utterly destroyed the imposing Egyptian army. Other Israeli units drove Syrian troops out of the Golan Heights, fended off Jordanian attacks, and captured the Old City of Jerusalem. "We have returned to our holiest of places," stated General Moshe Dayan,

defense minister of Israel, as he stood once again in the ancient city of Jerusalem, "never to be parted from it again."

By June 10, the Arabs agreed to a cease-fire. For the proud Arabs, even more devastating than their crushing defeat was their humiliation at the hands of the Israelis. In six short days, Israel had redrawn the map of the Middle East to its advantage. Israel occupied extensive Arab lands, including the West Bank of the Jordan River, the Golan Heights, the Gaza Strip, and the Sinai. The state of Israel grew from 8,000 square miles to 26,500 square miles, and 1 million Arabs became Israeli subjects.

The Rise of Sadat

Between the Six-Day War and 1970, sporadic conflict regularly broke the silence of the cease-fire. Egyptian commando units attacked Israeli military installa-tions. Artillery duels erupted across the Suez Canal, and the Israeli air force struck targets deep within Egypt. At the same time, the Soviet Union sent massive shipments of military supplies and 10,000 advisers to rebuild the Arab armed forces. In August 1970, however, Israel and Egypt agreed to another cease-fire.

The following month, Nasser died of a massive heart attack and Anwar Sadat became the new president of Egypt. Sadat eagerly took his self-appointed place as leader of the Arab crusade against Israel. From the beginning, Sadat wanted to break the stalemate with the Jewish state. He announced that 1971 was the "year of decision." If the dispute between Israel and the Arabs could not be settled peacefully, then Egypt would prepare for war. Sadat waited, but Israeli forces remained entrenched along the Suez Canal.

ASWAN HIGH DAM

Egypt's Aswan High Dam, one of the largest structures in the world, was completed in 1970. Located on the Upper Nile River, just south of the city of Aswan, the dam took ten years to build and cost $1 billion.

The United States and Great Britain had originally agreed to lend money to Egyptian president Gamal Abdel Nasser to finance the Aswan Project. They later withdrew their support because of Nasser's pro-Soviet policies. Nasser then secured Soviet aid to build the dam. Soviet premier Nikita Khrushchev traveled to Egypt for the opening ceremonies for the dam, one of his last international visits.

The Aswan High Dam provides irrigation and power to the Nile River region. The water it stores has opened up 900,000 acres of land, formerly desert, for cultivation. Its hydroelectric capabilities also supply half of Egypt's power.

GOLDA MEIR

Golda Meir served as Israel's prime minister from 1969 to 1974. A strong leader who emphasized foreign policy, Meir made it possible for many Soviet Jews to emigrate to Israel. She also strengthened Israel's ties with the United States and other nations. After retiring from public office in 1974, she wrote of her career, "There is a type of woman who cannot remain at home.... Her nature demands something more; she cannot divorce herself from the larger social life.... For such a woman there is no rest." Meir died in 1978.

▼ Several wealthy oil-producing states of the Middle East were also among the fastest growing in population.

It would be war, then. Sadat did not seek an all-out engagement with Israel. Rather, his goal was to force the Israelis to give back the Sinai. If the Egyptian army could recapture even a small part of the peninsula, Sadat thought, he could regain Arab prestige and force the Israelis to the bargaining table.

Both Syria and Jordan agreed to cooperate with Sadat's scheme. Throughout 1973, Sadat continued to buy military hardware, including advanced Soviet surface-to-air missiles that could shoot down Israeli jets. He also selected a date for a surprise attack on the Israeli positions: October 6, 1973.

The Yom Kippur War

October 6 was Yom Kippur, the Day of Atonement, the most important Jewish holy day. Sadat hoped the Israelis would be too occupied with prayer and fasting to respond to the Arab attack. His plan

worked—for a while. Although Israeli prime minister Golda Meir ordered the country's forces to prepare for war on the morning of October 6, it was two days before Israeli reserves were combat-ready. In the meantime, Egyptian troops surged across the Suez Canal under heavy artillery support, caught the Israelis off guard, and established a defensive position. Along the northern front, Syrian troops invaded the Golan Heights.

As soon as the Israelis began to counterattack, it became clear that they would not easily defeat the Arabs this time. The well-trained Israeli troops in the north were able to blunt the Syrian assault and retake the Golan Heights after several days of intense fighting. However, they were not able to destroy the Syrian army, which was supported by troops from Iraq and Jordan. The situation quickly became a standoff.

In the face of continuing assaults by the now-entrenched Egyptians, Israeli commanders in the Sinai executed a daring and risky maneuver. They sent troops across the Suez Canal to trap the two Egyptian armies from behind. The plan worked. When Sadat realized the situation, he called on the Soviet Union to arrange a cease-fire.

The Oil Embargo

Meanwhile, both the Arabs and the Israelis were in serious danger of losing the war unless they received additional weapons and ammunition. In response to pleas for help, the United States began to resupply Israel, and the Soviet Union began to resupply the Arab nations.

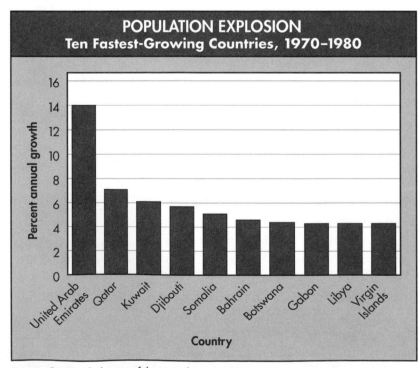

POPULATION EXPLOSION
Ten Fastest-Growing Countries, 1970–1980

Percent annual growth (y-axis: 0 to 16)

Countries (x-axis): United Arab Emirates, Qatar, Kuwait, Djibouti, Somalia, Bahrain, Botswana, Gabon, Libya, Virgin Islands

Country

Source: *Statistical Abstract of the United States, 1986.*

Then the oil-producing Arab nations introduced a dramatic new strategic weapon. Taking control over the price and supply of oil in their countries, they reduced or stopped oil shipments to the United States and all other nations supporting Israel. Through this **embargo** the Arabs hoped to pressure the United States and Western Europe into demanding Israeli withdrawal from all Arab land occupied since 1967.

With this international crisis as a backdrop, U.S. secretary of state Henry Kissinger went to Moscow to work out a cease-fire agreement. By the end of October 1973, all parties in the conflict except Syria had agreed to stop fighting. Israel and the Arab states also agreed to negotiate a long-term solution to their ongoing dispute. In March 1974 the oil embargo was lifted, much to the relief of oil-starved Western nations. But the price of oil had quadrupled in the meantime, affecting future international political and economic relations.

For many months Kissinger flew back and forth between the Israeli and Egyptian capitals, trying to negotiate an agreement. Finally, his "shuttle diplomacy" paid off. By January, Israel agreed to pull its forces back from the Suez Canal and allow United Nations troops to patrol a buffer zone between the two nations. Egypt agreed to reopen the canal to international traffic. In a second agreement, signed in mid-1975, Israel pulled farther back from the canal and Egypt agreed not to use force against Israel.

Negotiating an agreement between Israel and Syria was even more difficult. The two nations finally signed a cease-fire in May 1974, when Israel agreed to give back Syrian lands taken during the 1973 war. The UN also maintained a buffer zone in the region of the Golan Heights.

While the Middle East was now more stable and both sides showed more flexibility than in the past, Arabs and Israelis knew that hard work remained ahead to keep the peace. The stage was set for what would be the most stunning achievement of U.S. president Jimmy Carter: the historic 1979 peace treaty between Israel and Egypt.

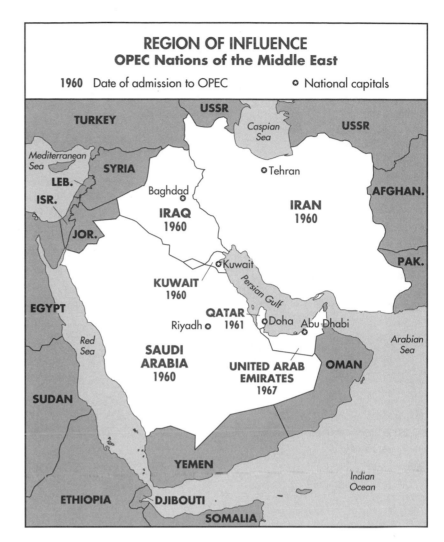

REGION OF INFLUENCE
OPEC Nations of the Middle East

1960 Date of admission to OPEC ⊕ National capitals

▲ The Organization of Petroleum Exporting Countries (OPEC) was formed in 1960 to give member countries more control over oil prices. OPEC includes these members outside of the Persian Gulf region as well (with dates of admission): Venezuela (1960), Indonesia (1962), Libya (1962), Algeria (1969), Nigeria (1971), Ecuador (1973), and Gabon (1973).

▼ The nearly complete Soviet and American pavilions competed for the world's attention at Montreal's Expo '67. The American building was a 20-story-high geodesic dome.

WESTERN HEMISPHERE NATIONS STRUGGLE FOR BALANCE

The people of the United States, according to the Mexican author Octavio Paz, "are always among us, even when they ignore us or turn their back on us. Their shadow covers the whole hemisphere. It is the shadow of a giant." For the nations of the Western Hemisphere, the United States can be a wealthy economic partner, a powerful political foe, or both. The story of the Western Hemisphere from 1964 to 1975 is the ongoing struggle to find a balance between cooperation and domination.

Canada

Between 1958 and 1962, Canada's ruling Conservative party seemed unbeatable. It had the largest parliamentary majority of any government in Canadian history. But an economic recession in the early 1960s took its toll. By 1963 the Liberal party under Lester Pearson, a Nobel Peace Prize winner, had taken control of the government. With Pearson at the helm, the Liberals pushed through an impressive program of social reform. In 1964 Canada adopted a national pension plan, and national health insurance was added in 1965. These two innovations provided sweeping income and health-care protection for all Canadian citizens.

A highlight of Pearson's term as premier was the spectacular Universal Exposition, or "Expo '67," held in Montreal to celebrate Canada's 100th anniversary as a nation. Expo '67 was the first world's fair to be held in Canada. In preparation for the Expo, the city of Montreal was redesigned and a new subway was built, one of the cleanest and safest in the world.

Visitors to the Expo noticed evidence of a deep fracture within Canadian society between people of British descent and those of French descent. Slogans such as "A Hundred Years of Injustice!" and "Long Live Free Quebec!" were scrawled on city walls. Many Canadians in the province of Quebec had long demanded separate status for their province. Jean Lesage, whose government led Quebec from 1960 to 1966, had as its motto "masters of our own house."

The **separatist movement** in Quebec was one of the first challenges confronting Pierre Elliott Trudeau, a French Canadian who

replaced Pearson as premier of Canada in 1968. The dilemma became even more acute when the Front for the Liberation of Quebec (FLQ), a radical separatist group, began a steady stream of terrorist activities designed to bring what they saw as freedom to Quebec.

Trudeau's response was twofold. First, he achieved passage of the Official Languages Act in 1969, which guaranteed government services in French to any area of Canada where at least 10 percent of the people spoke that language. Second, in response to two FLQ kidnappings, Trudeau sent 6,000 government troops into Montreal in 1970 to break the power of the terrorist organization. His tactics succeeded. Although the separatist movement remained an important political force in the early 1970s, it no longer threatened to break Canada apart.

Trudeau's other major challenge was the economic domination of Canada by its neighbor to the south. The U.S. economy was ten times the size of Canada's in the early 1970s; two-thirds of Canada's foreign trade was with the United States. Many Canadians felt that their economy was too dependent on the United States. When President Nixon imposed a new set of import taxes on foreign goods in 1971, Canada decided to take more control of its economic future. In that year, a development corporation was set up by Trudeau to buy control of foreign firms operating in Canada. In 1973 the Foreign Investment Review Agency was established to monitor and closely control all new foreign-owned companies doing business in Canada.

Also, as America searched for new sources of energy to replace embargoed oil in 1973, the importance to the U.S. economy of Canada's oil-rich and gas-rich western provinces soared.

Mexico

Like Canada, Mexico shares a long, undefended border with the United States. Also like Canada, Mexico's economy rises and falls with the U.S. economy. But the Mexican people, unlike the Canadians, have not enjoyed the same level of prosperity as the Americans. "When the U.S. sneezes, Mexico catches cold," according to a popular Mexican saying. When America suffers, Mexico suffers more. As **inflation** in the United States neared 10 percent in the mid-1960s, for example, Mexico's inflation rate soared to 20 or 30 percent.

Nevertheless, the 1960s were a period of impressive industrial growth in Mexico, which achieved one of the highest economic growth rates in the world. But, under the government of Gustavo Díaz Ordaz, only a relatively small group of Mexicans enjoyed the rewards of the new wealth. As inflation shot up and government repression of organized labor increased, discontent spread among Mexico's workers, intellectuals, and students. In 1968 the students went on strike to force a change, but the revolt was brutally crushed by government troops.

Political unrest and economic problems continued under Luis Echeverría Alvarez, who succeeded Díaz Ordaz as president of Mexico in 1970. Also, Mexico's relations with the United States deteriorated during Echeverría's six-year presidency. Echeverría maintained close ties with Fidel Castro in Cuba and Salvador Allende in Chile, both of whom were opposed by the United States. He also spoke out against the U.S. policy of intervention in Central America.

Mexico's economic fortunes improved in the mid-1970s, when one of the world's largest oil fields was discovered along the country's east coast. This new wealth raised hopes that Mexico's many social and economic problems could be solved.

Latin America

The 1950s and 1960s were decades of rapid industrial growth and economic expansion for many nations in Latin America. Industrialized nations sought Latin America's rich oil and mineral resources. Latin America's exports of coffee, sugar, and bananas were sold throughout the world. Even as Latin nations borrowed billions to develop their own economies, foreign companies built more and more factories in the region.

This heavy dependence on industrialized nations in Europe and North America had its price, however. When the world economy slumped, as it did during the mid-1970s, Latin American nations saw their earnings drop and their foreign debts soar. The situation grew even more serious when interest rates shot up in the late 1970s.

On the political front, the economic and social improvements in Cuba following Fidel Castro's 1959 takeover inspired people throughout Latin America to seek revolution and reform. Castro remained a thorn in the side of the United States—a sign the United States

▶ While American baseball, here played by Cuban president Fidel Castro (left), was extremely popular in the Caribbean, other American influences were not. U.S. paratroopers (right) landing at Santo Domingo, Dominican Republic, in 1965 found anti-American slogans all over the city. President Johnson sent troops to the Dominican Republic after the overthrow of its military government.

did not always have its way in the region.

It kept trying, however. In 1965 President Johnson sent troops to the Dominican Republic to thwart a Communist takeover. When Salvador Allende was elected president of Chile in 1970, the United States was determined to see that this Marxist was removed from office. In 1973 a CIA-sponsored military coup led by Augusto Pinochet seized power. But Pinochet's regime was so harsh that Congress cut off aid to Chile in 1975. Despite U.S. efforts to encourage Western-style democracy, many nations fell to military dictators during the 1960s and 1970s. Dictators took over eight nations between 1962 and 1964 alone. By the late 1970s, only four democracies remained: Costa Rica, Mexico, Colombia, and Venezuela.

WESTERN EUROPE GROWS STRONGER

During the first half of the twentieth century, two great wars and a global depression had ended Europe's political and economic dominance in the world. By 1975 the breakup of colonialism was nearly complete. Western Europe in the 1960s and 1970s strove to position itself in the shifting balance of world power through economic strength and political cooperation.

The Rise of West Germany

The economic recovery of West Germany following World War II

Che: Latin American Revolutionary

Che Guevara, a powerful Latin American guerrilla leader during the 1950s and early 1960s, was captured and executed by Bolivian army forces in 1967.

Born Ernesto Guevara in Argentina ("Che" was an Argentinian nickname), he became involved in leftist groups throughout Latin America. He joined Fidel Castro's revolutionary group in exile in Mexico and helped plan the overthrow of Cuban dictator Fulgencio Batista.

Guevara trained Castro's forces in guerrilla tactics. He quickly rose to the rank of major and led one of the forces that invaded central Cuba in 1958. After Castro's forces overthrew Batista in 1959, Castro appointed Guevara to several high government positions.

In 1965 Guevara left Cuba for his fateful trip to Bolivia to train a secret guerrilla force. His goal, to spread Castro's brand of communism throughout Latin America, was unsuccessful.

was nothing short of miraculous. Between 1950 and 1964, its GNP tripled and its exports increased fivefold. Its industrial growth was twice that of the United States, and it remained second only to America as a world leader in exports and auto production. One reason for West Germany's dramatic growth was its willingness to invest one-fourth of its GNP in new factories and equipment.

During this period, West German voters returned to the polls every four years to reelect the Christian Democratic party, led by Konrad Adenauer. When Adenauer retired in 1963, his economics minister, Ludwig Erhard, became the new chancellor. Not until the recession of 1966–1967 did West Germany's spectacular growth come to an end. Even then, the slump was short-lived. Erhard's government quickly pumped new **capital** into flagging industries,

TWO GERMANYS BEGIN DIPLOMATIC RELATIONS

With the election of Willy Brandt as chancellor of West Germany came new ideas regarding East Germany and the Soviet Union. Brandt's policy was called *Ostpolitik,* or "eastern policy." West Germany launched a series of treaties with East Germany, the USSR, and Poland.

As part of *Ostpolitik,* Brandt and East German prime minister Willi Stoph met in 1970. In 1972 the two German states agreed on a treaty that would control relations between them. Called the "Basic Treaty," this agreement recognized the postwar boundaries of the states and affirmed "each other's internal and external sovereignty." Although reunification was not discussed at that time, the Basic Treaty established a diplomatic framework that made future negotiations possible.

▲ East German premier Willi Stoph (right) greets Brandt in 1970 for the first summit talks since Germany split.

cial Democratic party. Brandt's commitment to democracy was legendary. After spending World War II in Norway, he returned to Germany, determined to help rebuild the shattered nation. "It would be better to be the only democrat in Germany than one of many in Norway or some other country where everyone knows what democracy is," Brandt wrote.

Chancellor Brandt unveiled a new "eastern policy" only a few weeks after he took office. His intention was to improve his country's relationship with Eastern European nations. In 1970 Brandt signed treaties with the Soviet Union and Poland recognizing the postwar borders of Europe. He recognized the legal existence of East Germany, and he helped arrange for easier access to West Berlin. Brandt's foreign policy was a sensational international success for which he won the 1971 Nobel Peace Prize.

Brandt unexpectedly resigned from office in 1974, when an official in his office was arrested on suspicion of spying for East Germany. He was replaced by Helmut Schmidt, who remained chancellor for the next eight years. Although the German economy was hit hard when world oil prices quadrupled in 1973, West Germany had sufficiently recovered by 1975 to be the leading economic power in Western Europe. It produced more goods and services than any nation in the world except Japan, the Soviet Union, and the United States. With foreign trade nearly equal to that of the United States, West Germany had risen again to become an economic superpower.

and soon the economy flourished once again.

In 1969 the 20-year reign of the Christian Democrats ended. The new West German chancellor was Willy Brandt, the leader of the So-

Nobel Peace Prize Winners, 1964–1975

Year	Winner	Description
1964	Martin Luther King Jr.	American clergyman and civil rights leader
1965	United Nations Children's Fund	———
1966	Not awarded	———
1967	Not awarded	———
1968	René-Samuel Cassin	French judge and chairman of UN Commission on Human Rights
1969	International Labour Organisation	———
1970	Norman Borlaug	American plant pathologist and geneticist
1971	Willy Brandt	German chancellor and diplomat
1972	Not Awarded	———
1973	Henry Kissinger	American political scientist and statesman
	Le Duc Tho	Vietnamese political leader
1974	Seán MacBride	Irish lawyer, politician, and United Nations official
	Eisaku Satō	Japanese premier
1975	Andrey Sakharov	Russian physicist and human rights activist

The Gaullist Republic in France

In May 1958, France faced its worst national crisis since World War II. French troops had suffered a humiliating defeat at the hands of Communist forces in Indochina. In addition, Muslims in Algeria had staged an insurrection against French rule. Fearing that France might leave Algeria to the Muslims, French settlers there threatened to march on Paris if France pulled out. The possibility of civil war loomed on the horizon.

In this moment of desperation, the French turned to the only man they believed could restore French unity: their wartime hero, Charles de Gaulle. On June 1, the National Assembly elected de Gaulle prime minister of France. After a new constitution was approved, de Gaulle was also elected president of France's Fifth Republic. He held both positions until 1969.

De Gaulle, a skilled communicator and charismatic orator, often ignored the French parliament. He chose instead to settle issues by popular vote. De Gaulle paved the way for Algerian independence. He also promoted an aggressive foreign policy based on a French-led Europe. To this end, he withdrew France from the North Atlantic Treaty Organization (NATO). He felt that the United States had too much control in NATO, a mutual defense organization created after World War II. De Gaulle also implemented domestic economic and social reforms, such as modernizing agriculture and improving the school system.

But the nation grew restless under de Gaulle's regime. Labor unions complained about inflation and lack of housing. Students at overcrowded universities called for the government to spend less on nuclear weapons and more on educational facilities. Opposition political leaders objected to the tight control of the mass media. In May 1968, student demonstrators in Paris clashed with police in the so-called Night of the Barricades that

▼ The withdrawal of France from NATO in 1966, engineered by French president Charles de Gaulle (left), sent American jeeps—and troops—to other locations in Europe. De Gaulle's goal of a more powerful and independent France also led him to block Britain's entry into the Common Market in 1967. France also developed its own nuclear weapons program.

► Barricades made of overturned cars were the remnants of several days of rioting in Paris in May 1968. The riots were followed by a five-week student occupation of the Sorbonne university in Paris and many workers' strikes.

ERA OF DICTATORS ENDS IN SPAIN AND PORTUGAL

By 1975 Spain and Portugal had entered a new political era. Generalissimo Francisco Franco, Spain's dictator since 1939, died on November 20, 1975. Two days later, his handpicked successor, Juan Carlos, was sworn in as king of Spain. Juan Carlos began to make plans for a parliament and free elections.

Portugal underwent similar transformations. In 1968, the Portuguese dictator Antonio Salazar suffered a stroke. Marcello Caetano replaced Salazar, who died two years later. In April 1974, a military coup began a revolution, and with it an end to totalitarian rule. Political parties were permitted, and free elections were held in Portugal in 1976—the first in over 50 years.

left 400 people injured. The revolt spread to universities across the nation, and soon workers joined the revolt. By May 25, almost 10 million workers were idle, and the future of de Gaulle's government was in serious question.

De Gaulle weathered the crisis only by promising reforms and an election in June, which resulted in an overwhelming majority for his party. The following year, however, de Gaulle lost a **referendum** on reform issues, and he resigned at the age of 78. He was succeeded as president by Georges Pompidou from 1969 to 1974 and Valéry Giscard d'Estaing from 1974 to 1981. Both continued, with few substantial changes, the policies of the Fifth Republic. Like most nations, France suffered from the effects of inflation, industrial slowdown, and unemployment in the mid-1970s.

For the most part, however, France enjoyed a politically calm period of relative prosperity.

Great Britain

When the Labour party took power in Britain after World War II, it began a series of reforms that made Britain one of the world's leading examples of parliamentary **socialism.** In addition to extending the pension, health, and unemployment benefits already in place, the Labour government created the National Health Service. It also brought under public ownership key segments of the British economy: the Bank of England, coal and steel production, electric and gas utilities, and communication and transportation industries.

In 1951, however, the Conservative party returned to power and governed until 1964. Champions of **capitalism,** the Conservatives returned many industries to private ownership. They did allow most health and social programs to remain, however. After 1964 the cycle of **nationalizing** and **privatizing** continued. With Harold Wilson as prime minister, the Labour party held office from 1964 until 1970, when power returned to the Conservatives under Edward Heath. Wilson gained office once again in 1974.

These rapid changes in leadership had little to do with varying opinions about socialism and capitalism among the British voters. Rather, the fortunes of the party in power rose and fell with the economy, which struggled during the period. The loss of colonial markets for manufactured goods, infla-

tion in the late 1960s, a lengthy and violent coal miners strike in 1972, the oil crisis in 1973—these events, along with a slow rate of industrial growth, left Britain's economy lagging far behind those of industrial rivals. By 1977 unemployment in Britain had reached more than 6 percent—the highest since World War II. Nearly 1.5 million workers were unemployed, and the British pound (its unit of currency) was worth less than at any time in history.

Two events provided bright spots in an otherwise gloomy picture. In 1973 Britain was invited to join the Common Market—a key economic and political European alliance. In 1975 Britain discovered a vast reservoir of oil below the ocean floor in the North Sea.

SUPERSONIC CONCORDE

On March 2, 1969, the first supersonic transport (SST), the Concorde, made its premiere test flight. The plane was capable of flying at twice the speed of sound—Mach 2, or 1,320 miles per hour.

A joint project of Great Britain and France, the Concorde was designed to carry 100 passengers and to cross the Atlantic in about three hours—half the time of conventional jets. The Concorde was put into worldwide passenger service in 1976.

Flights to the United States did not begin until 1978. American environmentalists were concerned about the effect of the SST on the earth's ozone layer, as well as the possibility of noise pollution from sonic booms.

Northern Ireland: A Bloody Conflict of Wills

The conflict between Catholics and Protestants in Northern Ireland did not begin in 1964, nor did it end in 1975. A million Protestants continued to insist that Northern Ireland remain part of Great Britain; half a million Catholics continued to want to unite with the Republic of Ireland.

The Home Rule Bill of 1920 had given the people of Northern Ireland considerable freedom to govern themselves. However, after Catholic civil rights protests in the late 1960s provoked violent Protestant attacks, British troops were sent to Northern

Ireland to restore order in 1969.

At the same time, the Irish Republican Army (IRA), which wanted all of Ireland united as an independent

▼ ▼ ▼

Despite occasional truces, the violent civil war, with its gun battles, terrorist bombings, and political assassinations, continued to tear Ireland apart.

nation, divided into two factions. The moderate arm was dedicated to political action, and the radical wing was devoted to terrorism. In re-

sponse to the British military presence, IRA radicals launched a murderous campaign of terrorism against both the British army and the Protestants.

Even with heavy reinforcements of British troops, the situation had deteriorated into a vicious stalemate by 1972. In an attempt to control the violence, the British government imposed direct rule on Northern Ireland. Despite occasional truces, however, the violent civil war, with its gun battles, terrorist bombings, and political assassinations, continued to tear Ireland apart.

THE SOVIET UNION'S HEAVY HAND

When Soviet economic woes and political rivalries within the Communist party unseated Nikita Khrushchev in 1964, he was replaced by two people. Leonid Brezhnev, a tough-minded Communist party leader, became general secretary of the party, and Aleksey Kosygin was named premier. Within a few years, however, Brezhnev had emerged as the dominant figure in both the party and the government. He ruled until his death in 1982.

The nation Brezhnev inherited from his predecessor still bore the unmistakable mark of Joseph Stalin's iron hand. Stalin had presided over industrialization in the 1930s, the defeat of invading German forces in the 1940s, and postwar reconstruction. By 1950 the Russian economy was poised to begin a 30-year period of impressive military and industrial growth. Progress under Stalin had come at dreadful human cost, however. His was a reign of terror; mass executions of opponents by the secret police were routine.

Brezhnev's style of governing differed from Stalin's only in degree. One historian put it this way: "Though the Chicago-style gangsterism of Stalin had been replaced by the low-key Mafia of Brezhnev and his associates, the essential criminality remained. The regime rested on a basis not of law but of force." Stalin himself once described the relationship between socialism—the official doctrine of the Soviet Union—and the power held by the ruling elite. "Don't talk to me about socialism," he said. "What we have, we hold."

Even so, the Soviet economy grew dramatically between 1950 and 1975. By the 1970s Soviet factories led the world in the production of cotton, steel, pig iron, coal, and oil. Agriculture was a glaring general exception to this trend. Harvest failures and low productivity made food rationing a frequent feature of Soviet life.

The Soviet people enjoyed few benefits from economic growth, however. Brezhnev poured vast sums of money into the production of weapons and military equipment, while only one-fourth of total economic output was devoted to consumer goods. By the time Brezhnev had been in power for 15 years, the Soviet workers' standard of living was about equal to that of American workers in 1920. But that was good enough for Brezhnev; he wanted no "revolution of rising expectations."

Firmly in control at home, Brezhnev also wielded considerable international influence. In a brutal display of force, he sent 250,000 troops into Czechoslovakia in 1968 to end a Czech move toward democracy. Following the invasion, Brezhnev stated what came to be called the "Brezhnev doctrine." It served notice that the Soviet Union would not "remain inactive" when East European countries in the Soviet bloc drifted away from communism. Ironically, a border dispute broke out the following year between the Soviet Union and China, the result of Mao's charge that the Soviets were

Terrorism: The Rising Global Threat

One of the Arab terrorists stands on a balcony of the Israeli Olympic team's dormitory.

In the early 1970s, the Soviet Union and the United States were trying to ease Cold War tension through **détente.** However, another political trend was taking its place— international terrorism. Around the world, renegade dictators and radical political groups employed random violence in a desperate attempt to gain through terror what they could not achieve otherwise. Most disturbing was the new choice of human targets: innocent civilians, chosen strictly on the basis of their symbolic value. Terrorists were willing to sacrifice anyone's life to bring their cause to the attention of the world community.

Individual acts of violence came from many different organizations: the Baader-Meinhof gang in West Germany, the radical wing of the Irish Republican Army in Ulster, the Red Brigades in Italy, Basque separatists in Spain, and the Palestine Lib-eration Organization (PLO) in the Middle East, among others. They used a number of tactics: bombing, assassination, shooting, massacre, and kidnapping. Hijacking airplanes was used often to gain maximum public attention with minimum risk to the terrorists. All acts of terrorism, no matter what their method or meaning, contributed to an international atmosphere of tension and foreboding.

Even more troubling, perhaps, was the dramatic increase in terrorism funded or carried out by national governments. The PLO had links to various members of the Arab League. The governments of Libya, Uganda, the Soviet Union, and Cuba were also known to have trained terrorists or paid for terrorist activities.

A terrorist attack during the 1972 Olympic Games in Munich, West Germany, dramatically illustrates the international horror and frustration generated by terrorism. In the predawn hours of September 5, 8 PLO guerrillas slipped into an Olympic Village dormitory and seized 11 Israeli athletes and held them hostage. The terrorists called themselves the "Black September" group, and they came well equipped with hand grenades and machine guns.

For 22 hours, a stunned worldwide audience watched their television screens as negotiations continued. The kidnappers demanded that Israel give up 236 "political prisoners" held in Israeli jails; Israel refused. West Germany wanted to avoid the killing of Jews on German soil, but they were determined not to allow the terrorists to leave the country.

Finally, West German and Israeli authorities devised a plan. They allowed the kidnappers and their hostages to be taken to an airport. Then West German authorities and the Israeli secret service attempted an ambush. In the ensuing disaster, all 11 hostages and 5 of their PLO kidnappers were killed. It was indeed a Black September in Munich.

not following communist doctrine closely enough.

Despite Brezhnev's displays of force, the Soviet need for U.S. technology and grain, combined with Nixon's new policy of détente (see The Nation), managed to thaw Cold War relations between the superpowers. When Nixon visited Moscow in 1972, he and Brezhnev signed a wide range of agreements on trade and technology. They also signed a breakthrough treaty designed to limit the number of strategic nuclear weapons held by the two nations.

Change and Crackdown in Eastern Europe

In 1955 six Eastern European nations—Poland, Hungary, Czechoslovakia, East Germany, Bulgaria, and Romania—joined the Soviet Union in forming the Warsaw Pact. Created to provide mutual defense, the organization quickly became a

▶ The Soviet invasion of Czechoslovakia in August 1968 took the world by surprise as it crushed the flowering of democratic reforms there.

vehicle for the Soviet Union to dominate the "satellite" nations that circled its borders. At various times, the fiercely self-reliant peoples of Eastern Europe tried to gain independence from their strict Soviet overlords. But, until the 1980s, they met with little success and much grief.

In 1956, for example, a popular uprising in Hungary threatened to bring down the Communist regime, cut ties with Moscow, and establish a parliamentary government. One leader of the rebellion congratulated the Hungarian people on "their glorious uprising" and warned the Soviets: "If your tanks enter Budapest, I will go into the streets and fight you with my bare hands." Khrushchev's tanks and artillery swiftly crushed the revolt.

Not all attempts at reform were ended so brutally. In 1968 Hungary managed to implement a "New Economic Mechanism" that used free-market forces to stimulate its sluggish economy. A 1970 uprising at the Gdansk shipyard in Poland (which would be the scene in 1980 of the birth of Solidarity) forced Communist party leaders to apologize for steep increases in food prices. "I am only a worker like you," a Communist official said, appealing to workers to help build a "second Poland."

The winds of change blew most freely through Czechoslovakia, however, during the remarkable "Prague Spring" of 1968. Alexander Dubček, leader of the Czech Communist party, wanted to leave behind the hard-line Soviet style of socialism. He sought to create "socialism with a human face" in his nation. Dubček spoke of the right to free speech and free assembly, citizen participation in decision making—a democratic form of communism. In this new environment, Czech writers and artists produced a steady stream of bold new plays, films, and literary works, demanding further reforms and more freedom.

It was a lovely spring, but the fall came quickly. On August 20, Warsaw Pact tactical air units and tank divisions clamped down on Czechoslovakia like a huge iron fist. Dubček was arrested, censorship returned, and reform activities were outlawed. Let this be a lesson to others who may stray, Brezhnev warned; the Soviet way is the only way.

CHINA OPENS UP

"Not to have a correct political point of view is like having no soul," wrote Mao Ze-dong (Mao Tse-tung), leader of China from 1949 until his death in 1976. The soul of every Chinese person, in Mao's view, was belief in a continuous people's revolution, one which would bring an ideal Communist utopia to China. Mao did not create the utopia he envisioned, but he achieved many of his goals.

After Mao's Communist party took control of China in 1949, he began to shape China into a unified, Communist nation. The process was never easy; often it was brutal and violent. "A revolution is not a dinner party," Mao said. "A revolution is an insurrection, an act of violence by which one class overthrows another."

By the mid-1960s, Mao had made huge advances in public health, literacy, population control, industrial growth, and the equality of women. The world's most populous nation was well on its way to becoming a modern industrial society. Yet Mao longed for a revolution that would transform the culture of China into a showcase of pure communism.

The Cultural Revolution

In August 1966, Mao began a ten-year social experiment, which he called the Cultural Revolution. He dispatched a million young students—his "Red Guards"—into towns and villages throughout China. Their mission was to "smash the old world" and "create a new world" by attacking the "four olds": old culture, old ideas, old customs, and old habits. The Red Guards set out with missionary enthusiasm, attacking Western literature, capitalist economics, Buddhist statues, traditional Chinese clothing, and everything else that deviated from strict Communist dogma.

What began as a campaign of posters and propaganda, however, quickly became a campaign of terror. "Political power grows out of the barrel of a gun," Mao once said, and the Red Guards took him seriously. They attacked all who opposed them; uncontrolled mobs threatened to rip China apart. The nation teetered on the brink of civil war.

By the time the violence subsided in 1969, as many as 400,000 people had died, and 3 million had been arrested and sent to labor

"From our past experience, we in China place immense hopes on the American people. They are a very great people with many different beliefs and races but, we believe, a common aspiration. Their potential and prospects are boundless."

—Chinese premier
Jou En-lai (Chou En-lai)

A contingent of Mao's Red Guards (holding a photo of the chairman) demonstrates in front of the customs house in Shanghai. Their attacks on anything smacking of private interest or Western influence created enormous upheaval in China during the Cultural Revolution. Many cultural links to China's past—artifacts and art treasures—were also destroyed.

STONE AGE TRIBE FOUND IN PHILIPPINES

Philippine officials stunned the world with their news in June 1971. They had discovered a small group of Stone Age people, the Tasaday, living in limestone caves deep within the rain forest. At the time of their discovery, the group of about 25 men, women, and children was living in complete isolation from civilization.

Anthropologists determined the Tasaday to be a primitive hunter-gatherer society. They knew nothing of agriculture, weaving, or pottery. Their clothing was made from leaves, and their tools were made from stone and bamboo. The Tasaday ate mostly wild yams, palm fruit, and small reptiles and crustaceans. Gentle and friendly, the Tasaday's social organization was strongly centered around the family.

In the late 1980s, scientific data suggested that the group was a hoax invented by the Philippine government. The issue remains unresolved.

camps. The economy and the educational system were a shambles. Mao was forced to compromise his revolutionary ideals to restore order. The Red Guards were sent back to school, and a shake-up of the Communist party allowed more practical leaders to begin the slow process of rebuilding the economy.

In the relative calm of the early 1970s, China displayed a new openness to the rest of the world, and vice versa. Pursuing his policy of détente, President Nixon sent his national security adviser, Henry Kissinger, on a top-secret trip to Beijing in July 1971. After Kissinger's meeting with Mao, the United States removed its opposition to China's membership in the United Nations. China was admitted to the UN in the fall. The following February, Nixon made a week-long visit to the People's Republic of China, which the United States had long considered a "Red menace." Spurred on by these diplomatic triumphs, China estab-

lished diplomatic relations with many other Western nations.

When Mao died in 1976, he was mourned as Father of the Revolution and hailed as one of the great leaders in China's history. He brought equality to China's peasants, freedom to its women, and respect for its workers. Under his leadership, China became a leading industrial and military power. But the cost of his revolution was brutal repression and uncontrolled violence, both of which left lasting scars on the people of China and their land.

GROWTH, STRIFE, AND SUFFERING IN ASIA

In the sixties and seventies, Asia and the Pacific islands were the focus of global attention for many reasons. Led by Japan, the region was becoming economically powerful. The trading cities of Hong Kong and Singapore flourished, and thriving Taiwan and South Korea became less dependent on aid from the United States. Asia was also the scene of national turmoil and Cold War conflict.

The Sun Also Rises

Like West Germany, the nation of Japan had suffered a devastating military defeat during World War II. But also like West Germany, Japan emerged in the postwar era to become an economic superpower. One reason for this prosperity was Japan's stable political atmosphere. Rivals of Japan's Liberal Democratic party had so little influence that some Japanese said theirs was a "one-and-a-half party system."

Despite its name, the Liberal Democratic party was staunchly conservative and enthusiastically probusiness. Much of the work of the government—preparing legislation, setting priorities, planning the budget—was done not by the elected National Diet (legislature), but by government ministries. For example, one Japanese official quipped that the budget "is not a political matter and politicians should not interfere with the government."

With the aid of careful government planning, the economy grew at a breathtaking rate: more than 10 percent a year from 1954 to 1972. Like other industrial nations, Japan suffered from inflation and industrial slowdown in the mid-1970s. But by 1975 Japan was the world's third-largest industrial power, the world's largest builder of ships, and a leading producer of cars, steel, and electronics equipment.

Japan's restriction of foreign imports within its borders caused increasing tension with its trade partners, including the United States. The United States believed Japan should be willing to import manufactured goods as freely as it exported them.

▼ As Japan's GNP rose, so did its exports to the United States. To American consumers in the 1960s, the label "Made in Japan" was usually seen on cheap gadgets and toys. By the early 1970s, though, the label applied to sophisticated consumer electronics, such as Sony color televisions.

AN ECONOMIC POWERHOUSE
Japan's Gross National Product, 1964–1975

Source: *International Financial Statistics Yearbook*, 1991.

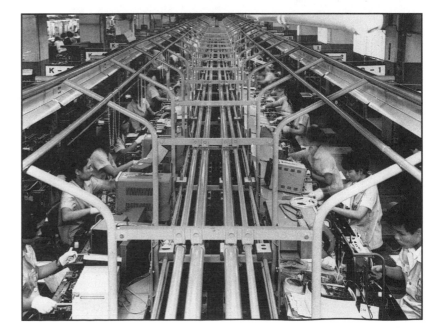

Progress and Strife in India

While China pursued its fevered drive toward pure communism, and Vietnam fought a raging war, India offered a refreshing example of political moderation in Asia in the 1960s. Ruled by a parliamentary democracy under the humane leadership of Jawaharlal Nehru, India was committed to solving its enormous social and economic problems: poverty, overpopulation, and ethnic diversity. Two years after Nehru died in 1964, his only child, Indira Gandhi, became the new prime minister and leader of the dominant Congress party.

Under Gandhi's leadership, India continued Nehru's plan for industrial and agricultural development, becoming nearly able to provide sufficient food for all its people. Even so, the skyrocketing increases in population constantly threatened to undo the progress that had been made. Gandhi also worked to make India a strong military power. By 1974 India had built an army of more than a million troops and had tested its first nuclear bomb.

The greatest challenge to India's influence in the region came in 1971, when the Bengali leaders of East Pakistan, which had half of

Indira Gandhi: New Spirit in Indian Leadership

Indira Gandhi, who had the same last name as Mohandas K. Gandhi, the revered leader of the Indian independence movement, was not related to him either by birth or in spirit. Like her father,

Jawaharlal Nehru, Indira Gandhi was far more successful with her foreign adventures than with her initiatives at home. In 1971 the government of Pakistan launched a strike against Indian air bases in its campaign to keep East Pakistan from gaining independence. In response, Gandhi immediately declared war on West Pakistan, defeated the Pakistani army, and gave the new nation of Bangladesh its independence.

The same year, Gandhi attempted to restructure India's financial system. When the courts declared her action **unconstitutional,** she dissolved parliament and led her party to an overwhelming victory in a new election.

Four years later, however, India's high court ruled that she had violated election laws in 1971. Undaunted, she declared a state of internal emergency and seized control of the government. She dismissed attempts by party leaders to question her authority. "When the great eagle flies under the stars," she declared, "the small birds hide."

Gandhi pursued an aggressive program of social reform, economic development, and forced birth control during the two-year period of emergency rule. But her often autocratic rule was her undoing. She went down to sweeping defeat in the 1977 elections. She returned as prime minister in 1980.

Pakistan's people but only one-sixth of its land, demanded independence from West Pakistan, located 1,000 miles away. West Pakistan sent troops to put down the rebellion; hundreds of thousands were killed. To end the bloodshed, India sent an army into the region, defeated the Pakistani troops, and forced recognition of the new nation, Bangladesh.

Southeast Asia's Suffering

It took the United States 9 years of intense fighting—and the South Vietnamese 11 years—to lose their all-out battle to contain communism in Southeast Asia. Despite America's military presence, the North Vietnamese could not be prevented from reuniting Vietnam under a Communist regime. The Vietnam War's battles spilled over into neighboring Laos and Cambodia. So did the consequences of America's defeat. By 1975 the worst fears of many Americans were realized: all of Indochina—Vietnam, Cambodia, and Laos—was in Communist hands.

In Cambodia, the Communist army, called the "Khmer Rouge," took the capital city of Phnom Penh in mid-April of 1975, the climax of their decade-long fight against the U.S.-backed Cambodian government. Under prime minister Pol Pot, the Khmer Rouge demanded "total social revolution" in Cambodia. They attempted, "through terror and other means," to strip away all signs of traditional Cambodian society and reconstruct it "according to party doctrines by substituting a new series of values."

This attempt to do in a few months what China had done in

The Father of Modern Vietnam

Ho Chi Minh was one of modern Asia's most influential leaders. Following World War II, Ho's Viet Minh (Vietnamese Independence Brotherhood League) fought a long war for independence from France. After they won independence in 1954, Vietnam was divided , and Ho ruled the North. He began fighting to reunify the country.

During the Vietnam War, Ho gradually turned over responsibility for running the North Vietnamese government to his loyal inner circle because his health was declining. He remained the symbol of a unified Vietnam, although he did not live to see that goal achieved. He died in 1969.

As a great patriot and liberation leader, and as founder of Vietnam's Communist party and its leader for 50 years, Ho Chi Minh is regarded by the people of Vietnam as the George Washington of their country. Saigon, once the capital of South Vietnam, was renamed Ho Chi Minh City.

25 years quickly turned into a national nightmare. Khmer Rouge forces massacred thousands of Cambodians, often without reason or purpose. By the time North Vietnam invaded Cambodia in 1979, more than a million Cambodians had died at the hands of the Khmer Rouge. An additional 4 million had lost their homes.

REVOLUTION AND INDEPENDENCE IN AFRICA

The year 1960 was a turning point for the people of Africa: 17 former colonies gained their independence. In most cases, the transition from colony to free statehood was orderly. But, for these and other African nations, the challenge of the 1960s was to weld diverse ethnic cultures into unified political and economic states. The road, as many nations discovered, could be rocky indeed.

A DANGEROUS YEAR IN INDONESIA

The year 1965 was turbulent for Indonesians. The country's economy was in bad shape. The authoritarian regime of Sukarno, who had been president since Indonesia won independence from the Netherlands in 1949, faced strong opposition from a growing Communist party and anti-Communist military leaders. In September, several Communist officers attempted to overthrow Sukarno. The coup was put down by rival forces led by General Suharto. During the four months that followed, Suharto's army massacred some 250,000 Indonesians who were thought to be Communists.

His popularity and authority badly eroded, Sukarno transferred political power to Suharto in March 1966.

Zaire

In 1959, after decades of Belgian control, the people of the Congo began to protest the presence of their European overlords. When the opposition to colonial rule erupted into violence, the Belgians suddenly agreed to withdraw. The Congo was granted independence in 1960, with only six months' preparation for self-rule. No political system existed to resolve the ethnic and regional differences, and conflict resulted. The new coalition government in the Congo faced a rising tide of riots, looting, and atrocities.

When Belgian troops in American planes returned to restore order, the USSR threatened to intervene in order to defend the new nation against capitalist domination. After several years of civil unrest and conflict between civilian and military rulers, Colonel Joseph Mobutu seized control of the government in 1965. A new constitution in 1967 gave him, as president, firm control over the nation.

Mobutu embarked on a program of economic reform that brought most of the nation's industries and businesses under public ownership. He also gave African names to all geographical features. The nation was renamed Zaire. Its capital, once called Léopoldville, became Kinshasa. Although regularly accused of corruption and human rights abuses, Mobutu brought stability to most of Zaire.

Nigeria

Nigeria, a former British colony, also gained its independence in 1960. Three years later, the four regions of Nigeria formed themselves into a federal republic. Because of its large population, the northern region was able to dominate the politics of the entire country. The Ibo people in the east, Nigeria's most advanced region economically, resented this control. In 1966 the tensions erupted into open violence, leading to a military coup in the east.

After a second coup six months later, the Ibo attempted to secede from Nigeria as the independent nation of Biafra in 1967. A bloody, two-and-a-half-year civil war followed. As many as 2 million Ibos died, either from the fighting or from malnutrition. Eventually, starvation and the superior might of the federal troops forced the Ibo to surrender.

After the civil war ended, the government of Nigeria tried to rebuild the nation's shattered economy and integrate the Ibo into national life once again. Even so, the military remained in control until 1979, when a new constitution and national elections transferred power to a civilian government.

Uganda

Winston Churchill called Uganda a "paradise on earth" after visiting the British colony. "It is a fairy tale: you climb up a railway instead of a beanstalk and at the top there is a wonderful new world," he said. Once considered the most beautiful nation in Africa, Uganda endured unspeakable horror and destruction during the 1960s and 1970s.

Uganda received its independence from Britain in 1962. But a struggle for power began almost immediately between the federal government and the centuries-old kingdom of Buganda, which had been promised self-rule within the new nation. Milton Obote, the prime minister, restored order only by making himself virtual dictator of Uganda. A narrow-minded and incompetent ruler, Obote was toppled in 1971 by Idi Amin Dada, his army chief of staff. Even then, Amin was known by his associates to be an exceptionally cunning and wicked man.

Once in power, however, his perverted character became horribly apparent to all. It almost speaks too well of Amin to describe his regime as a sadistic squad of racist, terrorist thugs. His minister of education, who fled in 1973, claimed Amin himself had "no principles, moral standards or scruples" and would "kill or cause to be killed anyone without hesitation."

Amin and his Russian-trained security forces massacred entire ethnic groups, and they tortured and dismembered their opponents. Amin even urged his subordinates to shoot anyone who displeased them. Uganda's once-prosperous agricultural economy completely disintegrated under Amin's dictatorship. The nation's nightmare did not end until Amin was driven from power in 1979.

Rhodesia

In the late 1950s and early 1960s, white settlers in the self-ruling British colony of Rhodesia came under heavy pressure from the British to give the black majority control of the government. In 1964 black-led governments established independent states in two regions,

now called Zambia and Malawi. But in Southern Rhodesia, the small white minority refused to surrender control over the region's 6 million blacks.

British officials tried to secure political rights for the black majority but failed. In 1965 Rhodesian prime minister Ian Smith made a unilateral declaration that Rhodesia was an independent nation, and the white-led government quickly adopted a constitution preserving white control. All nations except South Africa refused to recognize the new government, however, and the United Nations imposed economic sanctions to force Rhodesia to yield.

International pressure continued through the 1970s, and black guerrilla groups within Rhodesia kept the government from achieving complete domination. After 15 years, the Smith government was forced to relent, and the black-led state of Zimbabwe was formed in 1980.

▲ Idi Amin provoked international outrage in 1976 when he allowed a hijacked airliner to land at Entebbe, Uganda, and its Palestinian hijackers to detain the 98 Jewish passengers aboard. These hostages were rescued in a surprise raid by Israeli forces.

BUSINESS AND ECONOMY

In 1964 America had one of the strongest economies in the world. Unemployment was low and falling, personal income was high and rising, consumer prices were stable, and the gross national product was surging steadily upward. The nation exported about as many goods as it imported, and the federal deficit seemed under control. America's factories were productive and competitive. The products rolling off the nation's assembly lines were as well made as any in the world.

A decade later, the economic picture had changed dramatically. Financing the Vietnam War had pushed the federal government into serious debt. The Arab oil embargo resulted in long lines at the gas pumps and high

AT A GLANCE

- ► A Troubled Economy
- ► The Search for a Solution
- ► The Energy Crunch
- ► Consumerism and Environmentalism
- ► Workers Feel the Pinch
- ► American Business Loses Its Edge
- ► Still More Speed

gas prices. Personal income continued to rise, but so did inflation, unemployment, and interest rates. U.S. auto and electronics companies faced stiff competition from foreign manufacturers. Economists were busy trying to figure out how inflation could keep rising even as the economy slid into a recession—a situation economists called "stagflation" and everyone else called a disaster.

One political leader summed it up: "All the things that should go up—the stock market, corporate profits, real spendable income, productivity—go down, and all the things that should go down—unemployment, prices, interest rates—go up." The economy had turned into a giant puzzle, and a troubling one at that.

DATAFILE

Wealth and productivity	1964	1975
Gross national product	$632.4 bil.	$1.6 tril.
Per-capita income	$2,592.00	$6,081.00
Trade balance		
Imports	$28.7 bil.	$98.5 bil.
Exports	$37.3 bil.	$107.7 bil.
Dow-Jones average	891.71	881.81
Raw steel output		
(short tons)	127.1 mil.	116.6 mil.
Auto factory sales	7.8 mil.	6.7 mil.

Labor force	1964	1975
Total	75.8 mil.	93.8 mil.
Male	66.4%	60.0%
Female	33.6%	40.0%
Unemployment rate	5.2%	8.5%
Union membership	18.0 mil.	14.1 mil.

Government	1964	1975
Federal spending	$118.6 bil.	$332.3 bil.
National debt	$5.9 bil.	$53.2 bil.

MARKET BASKET
Retail Prices of Selected Items, 1969

Bread (1 lb.): **$0.23**

Three-minute phone call (New York to Denver): **$1.55**

Milk (½ gal., delivered): **$0.63**

Car (Toyota Crown): **$3,034.00**

Woman's dress: **$75.00**

Movie ticket: **$1.50**

Man's suit: **$115.00**

Eight-track stereo: **$59.95**

Postage (1st class, 1 oz.): **$0.06**

Electricity (per kilowatt hour): **$0.02**

Economy

A TROUBLED ECONOMY

In 1963 the **inflation** rate in America was 1.2 percent a year, a figure so low that almost everyone ignored it completely, economists and consumers alike. By 1974, however, inflation had increased to an annual rate of almost 11 percent. The nation was being battered by "the worst inflation in the country's peacetime history, the highest interest rates in a century . . . and a **stagnant** economy with large-scale unemployment," according to the *New York Times*. What had gone wrong?

Rising Prices

In 1964 Congress passed a $13 billion tax cut, a measure proposed by President Kennedy to stimulate the economy and pushed through by President Johnson. With extra cash in hand, American consumers went on a huge shopping spree. Demand for new products and services skyrocketed. As a result, the **gross national product** jumped from $573 billion in 1963 to $721 billion in 1966.

The buying binge was amplified when consumer credit cards began to flood the nation. Merchants had long since discovered that people spent more when they paid with credit cards—usually two to three times more. In 1965 BankAmericard (now Visa) and Master Charge (now MasterCard) began to issue credit cards nationwide. Within a year, there were 5 million bank credit cards in circulation; by 1974 the number had increased tenfold to 50 million.

▶ By the late sixties, credit cards were such a mainstay for business meals and expenses that a restaurant owner in downtown St. Louis felt it necessary to tell his customers, "We also accept cash."

Armed with plastic buying power, consumers charged everything from tooth extractions to tombstones. With demand strong, manufacturers and merchants were tempted to increase profit margins by raising their prices. Some did, although slowly at first. Wages also began to climb, as factory owners granted large wage settlements in order to keep assembly lines humming.

America began to buy something else on credit during the 1960s: the Vietnam War. President Johnson wanted to keep fighting the War on Poverty at home, but he also needed money for the war in Southeast Asia. During 1966, Johnson estimated that the Vietnam War would cost about $800 million a month. In fact, the war cost more than three times that amount. Because Johnson would not raise taxes to pay for the war,

MEDICARE ESTABLISHED TO HELP THE NATION'S ELDERLY

Congress established Medicare in 1965. The voluntary hospital and medical insurance plan for people aged 65 and older was originally proposed by President John F. Kennedy in 1963. Today more than 33 million people are enrolled in the Medicare program and receive total payments of about $90 billion a year.

the federal government was forced to borrow the difference—more than $20 billion a year. As the war dragged on, the federal **deficit** kept rising. The government used the funds to buy huge quantities of weapons, vehicles, and other supplies to fight the war, regardless of what they cost.

Thus, both American consumers and the federal government were spending vast sums of borrowed money during the late 1960s and early 1970s. The demand created by this spending spree pushed prices and wages ever higher. By 1969 a worried Nixon administration decided to slow the economic boom in order to curb inflation. Half the plan worked; after 105 months of steady growth, the economy went into a mild **recession**.

Petroleum Shock

The economists did not expect, however, that the inflation rate would continue its relentless climb—despite the recession. For the most part, however, the climb was slow and the rate of inflation remained manageable. Then, suddenly, the economy suffered a serious blow.

The Yom Kippur War, a fiercely fought struggle that pitted Israel against Egypt and Syria, erupted in 1973 (see The World). During the war, Arab nations tried to use their supply of oil to prevent Western nations from supporting Israel. In October, Saudi Arabia placed an **embargo** on oil shipments to Israeli allies, including the United States. The oil-thirsty U.S. economy went into shock. Oil-fired generating plants were forced to decrease their production of electricity, causing "brownouts," or loss of power, in some areas. Gasoline and heating oil were in short supply, and many workers in oil-dependent industries were laid off.

To make matters worse, the Organization of Petroleum Exporting Countries (OPEC) decided to raise oil prices and set production quotas. By January 1974 the price of crude oil had quadrupled throughout the world, and strict limits on production kept prices high. American oil companies benefited greatly from the increase in oil prices. With no incentive to keep prices down, they made very large **windfall profits** during the crisis. The effect of the actions of OPEC and the U.S. oil companies on the U.S. economy was immediate and severe. The inflation rate jumped to 11 percent, industrial production plummeted, and unemployment rose. In other words, the economy was in a recession, the most serious since the Great Depression of the 1930s.

The Great Recession

It had always been one of the fundamental truths of economics: inflation and stagnation are like oil and water—they do not mix. Sometimes prices and wages rise, and sometimes industrial production slows down, but they never happen at the same time. Wages and prices go up when demand for new products is high, and high demand boosts production. That's what everyone thought until the early 1970s.

The puzzle of the recession during 1974–1975 was the presence of stagflation, which is the combination of stagnating growth and rising inflation. The decline in industrial productivity was caused by two different factors. As prices continued to climb, American consumers found they could buy fewer and fewer items with their money. This situation led to an overall decline in consumer demand for new products.

At the same time, U.S. factories, once world leaders in worker output, had fallen to last in productivity among industrial nations. Outdated U.S. factories couldn't compete with companies in West Germany and Japan that were using new, less costly production technologies. Also, most U.S. companies were not willing to update their product lines to give Americans the goods they wanted at reasonable prices. Detroit, for example, kept producing large cars that got very poor gas mileage. Because foreign companies were producing high-quality goods at low prices, Americans bought more and more imported autos, electronic goods, and other items. The

▲ OPEC nations meet in Algiers, Algeria, for a 1975 summit.

GAS CRISIS UPSETS AMERICAN MOTORISTS

The Arab oil embargo created long lines at gas stations across the country during the winter of 1973–1974 as drivers panicked that the supply would run out. Some people had to wait hours just to fill their tanks. Gas stations began to ration gasoline, selling to drivers with even- and odd-numbered license plates on alternating days. Some stations were forced to close when their tanks ran dry.

Drivers sometimes resorted to violence. Heated arguments at the pumps were common. A few drivers threatened gas station employees with guns. Although the embargo was lifted in 1974, the effects of rising oil prices lasted for many years.

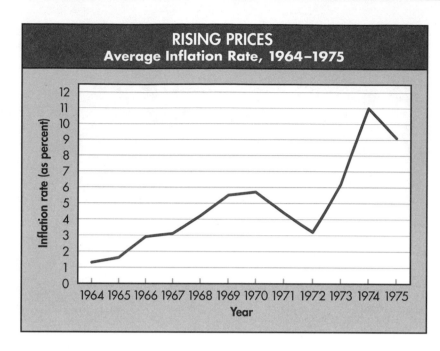

RISING PRICES
Average Inflation Rate, 1964–1975

Inflation rate (as percent) vs Year (1964 1965 1966 1967 1968 1969 1970 1971 1972 1973 1974 1975)

▲ The wage-price controls of 1971–1972 lowered the inflation rate, but led by rising food and energy prices, the rate soared in 1973.

▼ Japan's share of the U.S. auto market more than doubled in the first half of the 1970s. By 1990 it had climbed to 18.5 percent.

demand for U.S. products dropped even lower.

However, by 1974 inflation remained in double digits, even as unemployment soared. One of the reasons prices remained high was that companies had to cover their increased production costs, including the high price of energy and raw materials.

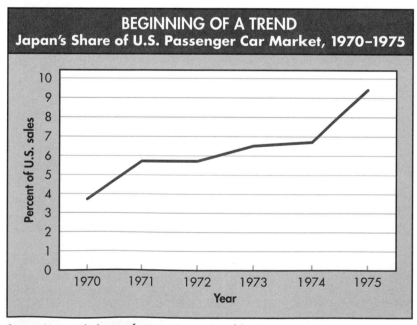

BEGINNING OF A TREND
Japan's Share of U.S. Passenger Car Market, 1970–1975

Percent of U.S. sales vs Year (1970 1971 1972 1973 1974 1975)

Source: Motor Vehicle Manufacturers Association of the U.S., Inc.; Ward's Automotive Reports.

THE SEARCH FOR A SOLUTION

When Richard Nixon took office in 1969, inflation stood at about 6 percent, the result of "the total growth of spending" by both government and consumers, according to Nixon. The new president promised to reduce spending, shrink the money supply, and raise certain taxes—a strategy designed to cut inflation by slowing the economic boom. Labor leaders and business managers, on the other hand, "have to be guided by the interest of the organization they represent," stated Nixon. To some observers, this comment by Nixon gave businesses the go-ahead to raise prices.

In the months that followed, the nation endured what Nixon called "slowing pains." In 1970 the gross national product dropped for the first time since 1938 and interest rates climbed to their highest level in a hundred years. Unemployment stood at 6 percent, and the stock market was dropping like a stone. A hundred brokerage firms were on the edge of bankruptcy, and the Penn Central railroad was on the brink of becoming the biggest business failure in world history. Even so, inflation continued its relentless climb.

Yet Nixon held firm. "I will not take this nation down the road of wage and price controls," he vowed, because "they rob every American of an important part of his freedom." He broke his vow on August 15, 1971, when the persistence of inflation forced him to announce a new economic policy. This policy imposed a 90-day freeze on all wages, prices, and profit margins. The stock market responded enthusiastically, but labor leaders were not happy.

To boost the nation's foreign trade, Nixon also took the United States off the gold standard; the country stopped converting dollars into gold. In 1971 and again in 1973 the United States signed international agreements to reduce the value of the dollar in relation to foreign currencies. These moves lowered the cost of American goods to foreign buyers, but they did not deal with the underlying problem. Stiff competition from efficient foreign manufacturers continued to eat away at the market share of U.S. industries both at home and abroad.

After Nixon was reelected in 1972, he predicted that the next two years would be "the best years our economy has ever experienced." In January 1973 he replaced the wage and price freeze with a set of voluntary guidelines. Many economists disagreed with the president's action, believing instead that the situation called for price and wage controls to remain.

The economists proved correct. Inflation climbed once again to almost 10 percent during the first five months of 1973. Runaway food prices—they rose an average of 15 percent in 1973—led angry consumers to declare a **boycott** on meat in April. In June, the president reluctantly imposed a 60-day freeze on prices. However, even Nixon conceded that food prices would rise substantially "with or without price controls." By August,

Nixon had devised a complicated system of modified price controls linked to cost increases. However, the oil embargo in October ended any hope that Nixon's new economic plan would work.

When the Watergate crisis forced Nixon to resign, Gerald Ford

The Fed and Inflation

The U.S. economy is a hugely complex financial system made up of an intricate network of institutions and individuals. Dauntingly hard to understand, the economy is even more difficult to control.

In some ways, money is like any other commodity in a market economy. When the supply of money is plentiful, its price—the interest rate—goes down. If money is in short supply, the interest rate goes up. But, unlike other commodities, money can be created not only by printing actual dollar bills but also by extending more credit. That is where the Federal Reserve System ("the Fed") comes into the picture.

The Fed, which is our nation's central bank, can influence the size of the money supply by changing the interest rate it charges for lending money to the coun-

try's commercial banks. If it raises rates, banks and their customers will borrow fewer dollars, reducing the overall money supply. In normal economic times, raising interest rates and reducing the money supply—making money more expensive, in other words—encourages people to spend less. And when less money chases the same quantity of goods, prices remain steady and inflation stays low.

▼ ▼ ▼

The Federal Reserve can influence the size of the money supply by changing the interest rate it charges to banks.

As economists and presidents discovered during the 1970s, however, those were not normal economic times. Despite the efforts of the Fed, inflation climbed anyway.

Juanita Kreps, First Woman to Head the Commerce Department

Juanita Morris Kreps is a distinguished economist and professor of economics. Her economic research and writings have focused on the employment problems of women and older workers. She taught economics at Duke University from 1955 to 1977. From 1973 to 1977 Kreps also served as vice president of Duke. In 1972 while at Duke, Kreps became the first woman to be elected to the board of directors of the New York Stock Exchange.

In 1977 Kreps was chosen by President Jimmy Carter to be secretary of commerce. She was the first woman and the first professional economist to serve in that post. As secretary of commerce, Kreps sought to represent the interests of the public as well as those of business leaders.

After her service in Carter's Cabinet, Kreps returned to Duke University.

took up the crusade to combat inflation. In the face of continued price increases, Ford presented his plan to "WIN: Whip Inflation Now." He called for the Federal Reserve to raise interest rates, which would encourage both the government and consumers to reduce spending. A drop in demand, Ford hoped, would cause a surplus of goods and lead to a drop in prices. To curb government spending, Ford vetoed new funding for housing, health, and education.

Ford's WIN program made modest progress toward its main goal. Inflation dropped to 9 percent by 1975 and 6 percent by 1976. Along with progress against inflation, however, came economic chaos in other areas. As consumer demand fell, manufacturers cut back their production, and more and more workers lost their jobs. By 1975 almost one in ten American workers was unemployed. Even though the unemployment rate dropped to 7 percent in 1976, Americans were still dissatisfied with the state of the American economy. In the November presidential election, they voted President Ford out of office in favor of Jimmy Carter, a former governor of Georgia and relative newcomer to national politics.

Energy

THE ENERGY CRUNCH

In January 1971 the price of Arab light crude oil stood at $1.80 per barrel on the world market. Three years later, Arab light crude was selling for the then-unheard-of price of $11.65 a barrel. This sixfold leap in prices had a variety of causes:

▶ OPEC placed an embargo on oil shipments to Israel's allies during the 1973 Yom Kippur War.
▶ OPEC raised oil prices and set production quotas after the Yom Kippur War.
▶ The Nixon administration decided to lower the value of the dollar in relation to foreign currencies.
▶ American oil companies cut domestic production in the early 1970s.

Whatever the cause of these increases, their short-term effect, combined with a widespread shortage of petroleum products, came as a rude shock. Americans had been freely using gas and oil to fuel their cars and heat their homes.

The nation made up only 6 percent of the world's population, but it consumed about a third of the world's energy. Americans used 9.7 million barrels of oil per day in 1960 and 14.4 million in 1970. By 1974 consumption had reached 16.2 million barrels per day. As a result, the percentage of oil imported from foreign countries doubled between 1960 and 1974, to 38 percent of all oil used in the country.

The energy crunch of the early 1970s sent a clear message to all Americans. The nation was consuming far too much energy for its own good, and far too much of its energy supply came from undependable foreign sources. Would the nation hear the message and take action to prevent another energy crisis in the future?

Nixon sent his first message on the nation's energy policy to Congress in June 1971. The president ignored the looming threat of OPEC and the critical issue of foreign oil. Instead, he called for new advances in "clean energy" sources, such as nuclear reactors and coal gas. By the winter of 1973–1974, however, it became obvious that more comprehensive proposals would be needed.

In April 1973 Nixon made another energy address to Congress. Ignoring the protests of environmental groups, he promised to lease more offshore land for oil drilling, open Alaska to further energy development, and ease strip-mining standards. He also demanded quick approval of the Alaskan oil pipeline and declared that nuclear energy was the nation's "major alternative to **fossil**

fuel energy for the remainder of this century." To carry out his initiatives, Nixon created the Federal Energy Office.

The OPEC oil embargo pushed the president even further. We must now confront "a very stark fact," warned Nixon; "We are heading toward the most acute shortage of energy since World War II." In response to the worsening crisis, Nixon launched his "Project Independence," which he heralded as "a major new endeavor" to make the United States independent of foreign energy sources by 1980. Nixon reminded the people that the same national commitment that put America on the moon in the 1960s could make America energy-independent in the 1970s.

The main features of Nixon's program were rapid, large-scale increases in coal production and nuclear energy. Conservationists protested that Nixon's plans would lead to massive strip-mining for coal and to pollution of the land

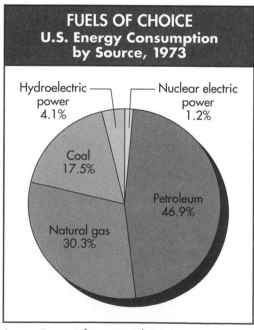

FUELS OF CHOICE
U.S. Energy Consumption by Source, 1973

Hydroelectric power 4.1%
Nuclear electric power 1.2%
Coal 17.5%
Petroleum 46.9%
Natural gas 30.3%

Source: Energy Information Administration.

◀ In 1973 nearly all U.S. energy consumption came from fossil fuels—petroleum, natural gas, and coal.

► In late 1973 President Nixon asked Congress to lower the maximum speed limit on the nation's highways to 50 miles per hour to conserve gasoline. Some states, such as Vermont, reduced their top speed immediately. After protests from truckers, however, Congress established a maximum of 55 miles per hour. Though this measure was at first temporary, significant fuel savings and a drop in highway deaths led Congress to make the limit permanent the next year.

RECYCLING BEGINS TO HAVE AN EFFECT

In the late 1960s glass manufacturers established recycling centers in an effort to reduce litter and protect the environment. Consumers were asked to bring their glass bottles and jars to these centers so that the manufacturers could turn the containers into new bottles and jars. With this method, glass containers could be reused 40 to 50 times.

A few states passed laws that restricted the use of nonreturnable beverage containers. Oregon enacted the first such "bottle bill" in 1972. In just a few years, roadside litter in Oregon had been dramatically reduced.

In 1970 people were generating over 12 million tons of glass waste a year. Just 2 percent of the glass was able to be recycled. By the late 1980s the amount of glass waste had increased by only 200,000 tons a year, and almost 9 percent of the glass was able to be recycled.

and water. Nevertheless, Congress and the energy industry proceeded with Nixon's agenda.

The Emergency Petroleum Allocation Act raised the price of domestic oil to stimulate production and gave new powers to the federal energy director. By January 1974, 42 nuclear power plants were operating, 56 were under construction, and orders had been placed for 100 more. Nixon ordered Americans to set thermostats at 68° Fahrenheit and drive at 55 miles per hour. He called for reductions in air travel and increased use of car pools and mass transit.

Unfortunately, the nation's fervor to conserve energy and find alternate fuels was short-lived. By the time a disgraced Nixon resigned in August 1974, the OPEC embargo had ended and the supply of oil had returned to normal.

Even though prices remained high, many Americans stopped worrying about the problem of energy dependence. They reset their thermostats, started buying large cars again, filled up their gas tanks, and ignored the new 55-mile-per-hour speed limit. Many plans for pursuing alternative sources of energy and for increasing domestic oil, gas, and coal production were set aside. The crunch had temporarily passed.

Business Issues

CONSUMERISM AND ENVIRONMENTALISM

Beginning in the sixties, the concerns that many Americans were voicing about consumer protection, workplace safety, and environmental problems began to have an impact on big business and government.

During the period between 1964 and 1975, both public and private consumer advocates came on the scene and began to exert influence. President Johnson, for example, enlarged the Consumer Advisory Council and made it part of a Committee on Consumer Interest. In the mid-1960s Ralph Nader emerged as a tireless defender of American consumers against defective and unsafe products. The Consumer Federation of America was made up of 56 organizations when it was formed in 1967. Within three years, its membership had grown to 179 groups. The formation of the Consumer Product Safety Commission in 1972

marked the start of a new era of government activism on behalf of American consumers.

Through these new voices, consumers called for American corporations to consider people before profits. Once, American businesses could measure their progress by looking solely at the bottom line. By 1975 they had to evaluate the effect of their operation on the environment. They also had to consider the safety of their products to consumers. At the same time, workers made known their concerns over safety on the job. As a result, the Occupational Safety and Health Administration (OSHA) was founded in 1970 to set and monitor safety regulations in the workplace.

In the early 1960s most Americans believed in the progress of American technology. By the end of

Ralph Nader: An Advocate for the American Consumer

Once in a while, someone proves that one person can make a difference. One such person was Ralph Nader. He was determined to save American consumers from harm by uncaring corporations. A graduate of Princeton University and Harvard Law School, Nader made no compromises in his quest to expose unsafe products and ensure fair treatment of consumers.

Nader first gained national attention in 1965 with his book *Unsafe at Any Speed*. In it, Nader argued that defective designs in cars built by the nation's automakers had caused many accidents and injuries. The auto industry was furious. General Motors hired a private detective to "get something on this guy . . . get him out of our hair . . . shut him up." The detective found nothing, but Nader found out about the investigation and sued for invasion of privacy. He settled the suit when the automaker agreed to make a public apology and give him $500,000, which he poured into his crusade. Despite the efforts of the auto industry, Nader's testimony before Congress resulted in the 1966 National Traffic and Motor Vehicle Safety Act, which led to padded dashboards, headrests to prevent whiplash, safety glass, seat belts, and other safety features.

This initial success gave Nader instant access to members of Congress. He then often gave expert testimony to congressional committees on consumer issues. Nader's revelations led to the Wholesome Meat Act (1967), the Natural Gas Pipeline Safety Act (1968), and the Radiation Control for Health and Safety Act (1968).

By 1968, Nader had gathered a group of college

students, who were nicknamed "Nader's Raiders," to examine the work of government regulatory agencies. Before long, these activities were made part of his newly formed Center for the Study of Responsive Law. In 1971 Nader founded Public Citizen, Inc., a consumer lobbying group. By that time corporations and government agencies knew that he was a force to be reckoned with.

the decade, however, the by-products of progress—toxic industrial waste, runoff of agricultural chemicals, exhaust from burning fossil fuels—had seriously polluted the nation's land, water, and air. People began to question the meaning of this progress. Why have a weekend house on the lake, they asked, if the water is so polluted that no one can swim in it? What is the benefit of buying new appliances if generating electricity to run them makes the air unbreathable?

The financial costs of cleaning up the environment were high for both government and industry. Each new law designed to reduce pollution, safeguard the environment, and protect consumer rights increased the cost of providing goods and services to American consumers. However, the cost of pollution to the quality of life became too obvious to ignore in the late 1960s and early 1970s.

As early as 1964, President Johnson included environmental initiatives in his ambitious campaign to create a Great Society. "The water we drink, the food we eat, the very air that we breathe, are threatened with pollution," he declared. "Our parks are overcrowded, our seashores overburdened. Green fields and dense forests are disappearing."

Johnson's agenda sought to improve the quality of American life in a number of areas. For example, the Wilderness Act of 1964 set aside 9 million acres of federal land as wilderness, safeguarding them from development. That same year, the Public Health Service linked cigarette smoking to several deadly diseases. In 1965 Congress passed legislation limiting billboards and junkyards along federal highways.

The Johnson administration also pushed through an updated Clean Air Act. The Clean Air Act of 1963 had provided federal money and technical help to state and local pollution-control agencies. The second Clean Air Act, passed in 1967, set tough new standards designed to limit air pollution by smokestack industries. This action followed a Thanksgiving Day tragedy in 1966, when 168 people in New York City died from a severe episode of air pollution.

President Nixon, although sympathetic to the concerns of industry, approved additional legislation designed to protect the environment. "It's now or never," he declared. "America pays its debt to the past by reclaiming the purity of its air, its waters, and our living environment." That said, Nixon signed a bill that became the National Environmental Policy Act of 1969, which made the government directly responsible for maintaining a safe environment. The act also required government agencies to complete environmental impact studies before any public project could be approved. Nixon was also responsible for creating the Environmental Protection Agency by executive order in 1970 and for signing a Great Lakes Water Quality Agreement between the United States and Canada. About the same time, the Department of Agriculture severely restricted the use of the pesticide DDT, after almost a decade of public controversy provoked by Rachel Carson's 1962 book *Silent Spring*.

WORKERS FEEL THE PINCH

From 1964 to 1975 labor in the United States underwent many changes. The workforce was affected by the uncertain economy, the increase in automation, and civil rights legislation.

Union Consolidation

During the 1960s union membership continued to grow but at a much slower rate than the labor force. Between 1956 and 1967, for example, union membership

---

César Chávez, Farm Workers' Advocate

> **NOTICE:**
> **California Grape Boycott**
>
> United Farm Workers led by César Chávez are calling for a boycott of California table grapes. . . . It is this grocer's current policy to inform consumers of the boycott request so that each consumer can make his or her own purchase decision. It's your decision—to boycott or not.

If you had walked into any grocery or supermarket during the late 1960s, chances are you would have seen this notice or one like it. If not, you surely would have read news of the boycott in the newspaper or heard about it on radio or television. Everyone knew that the United Farm Workers (UFW) union was asking consumers to support the right of the union to be recognized by the grape growers. Many consumers read the notices and made their decisions. Many left the grapes in the produce aisle.

The grape boycott was organized by a "quiet explosion" named César Chávez.

The son of a migrant farm worker, Chávez knew well the hard life of workers—most of whom were Hispanic like him—who moved from one farm to the next, planting and harvesting labor-intensive crops such as grapes and lettuce. Chávez himself had attended more than 30 elementary schools as a youngster. He grew up quietly determined to help improve the pitifully low pay and abysmal working conditions endured by many farm workers.

Chávez began organizing farm workers in 1962. At first, he was opposed by both the growers and the Teamsters Union, which had been given permission by the growers to represent farm workers. The successful nationwide boycott of table grapes led by Chávez soon gained recognition for the United Farm Workers and increasing respect for this soft-spoken labor leader. Chávez's union helped migrant workers get U.S. citizenship, register to vote, and get loans. The union also provided a health clinic.

Unlike many union leaders of the period, Chávez based his tactics on the nonviolent philosophy of India's Mohandas K. Gandhi and of Martin Luther King Jr. "If someone commits violence against us, it is much better—if we can—not to react against the violence, but to react in such a way as to get closer to our goal," Chávez later wrote. And he did reach his goal: boycotts of grapes, lettuce, and citrus fruits forced growers to sign contracts with the UFW. By 1972 more than 60,000 farm workers had joined the union.

TEACHERS' STRIKE DIVIDES NYC

In 1968 the National Education Association reversed its position against teachers' strikes when it backed a three-week walkout in Florida, the first statewide teachers' strike. That same fall, national attention focused on New York City when a strike by the United Federation of Teachers (UFT) closed city schools for three weeks.

One of the main issues of the New York City strike was a controversial new structure for the school board. Under the experimental plan, locally elected community boards gained increased control over the schools in their neighborhoods.

Most of the teachers of the predominantly black inner-city schools were Jewish. When the community board for these areas tried to transfer some teachers and replace them with others, the teachers accused the board of anti-Semitism. The teachers, supported by the UFT, went on strike as a protest. The unpopular strike divided the community even more. In response, the New York legislature decided to end the community board plan.

increased by only 400,000 workers, while the nonfarm workforce grew by more than 11 million. However, during this time, the numbers of blacks and Hispanics who joined unions grew. The growth was partly a response to the Equal Opportunity Act and the Civil Rights Act of 1964, which ordered unions to open membership to minorities. Also during this period, federal government workers and many state and local government employees were permitted to unionize. Teachers, postal workers, garbage collectors, and others took advantage of this right.

Substantial pay increases for union members were common during the period, especially when the inflation rate reached double digits. In 1971, for example, railroad workers received a 46 percent pay increase spread over three and a half years. As a result, union negotiators began to focus on another problem for many workers: job security. In 1964 the U.S. Labor Department reported that 200,000 jobs were being lost each year because of automation. Many of these jobs were in the auto, steel, railroad, and mining industries—traditional union strongholds. When the recession hit the economy in the early 1970s, layoffs increased even more. Unemployment hit a high of almost 9 percent in 1975.

Workforce Changes

The slow but certain shift in organized labor was driven by broader trends within the economy. Over the period, new technology continued to reduce the overall demand for blue-collar workers. At the same time, most new jobs required white-collar and other salaried workers, who proved less inclined to join unions than their wage-earning colleagues. The number of farmers also declined dramatically; more than a million family farms were lost during the 1960s.

During this period, two-income households became common, as more and more women joined the workforce to help their families combat the effects of inflation. Overall, the income of black workers increased substantially during the 1960s and 1970s, even though they were especially hard hit by unemployment.

Commerce

AMERICAN BUSINESS LOSES ITS EDGE

American businesses faced serious setbacks between 1964 and 1975. Inflation rose to an annual rate of 11 percent in 1974, and the gross national product dropped in 1970 for the first time in 32 years. At the same time, new government regulations increased the cost of industrial production, and competition from cost-efficient foreign manufacturers made sizable inroads into U.S. markets. It was a tough time to be in business in America.

An International Economy

The term *global economy* was heard with increasing frequency in the nation's business centers during the 1960s and 1970s. One reason was the rapid increase in the number of **multinational** corporations—companies that do business in a number of different countries. Many American corporations, for example, built factories in the Far East or established regional headquarters in Europe. In this way, businesses could take advantage of low foreign labor costs while expanding the market for their products.

American banks also caught the international fever. Flush with cash from overseas depositors, large private banks made huge loans to developing countries in South America, Asia, and Africa. This trend reached its peak during the early 1970s, when OPEC nations reaped vast profits from raising oil prices and put the money into Western banks. When the global economy went into a slump and interest rates soared in the late 1970s, however, many developing nations were unable to repay their loans. As a result, the banks lost money.

A National Crisis

The flurry of international activity reflected a serious problem that continued to plague American industry, especially during the 1970s. Many companies decided not to invest capital to build and improve factories in the United States but to build overseas manufacturing plants instead. They did this for two reasons.

First and foremost, foreign employees were paid far less than American factory workers, many of whom belonged to powerful labor unions. In many cases, companies did not provide health and medical benefits overseas, nor did they pay overtime. Often, labor costs in for-

eign factories were one-fourth those in America.

Second, foreign nations usually had fewer regulations concerning worker and environmental safety. American businesses complained bitterly about the cost of complying with federal government rules set down to protect the environment and to ensure worker safety. Simply put, fewer rules meant more profits.

In the 1970s however, this international trend had a devastating impact on American businesses and workers. Factories became outdated. They were unable to compete with foreign manufacturers, who often used advanced technology and automated plants. As a result, demand for American-made products declined sharply, both here and abroad. In 1971 the value of products imported by the United States exceeded the value

▲ In 1968 New York's Citibank unveiled its first automated cash machine. Like modern electronic tellers, this test machine dispensed cash after the customer inserted a plastic card and punched in a code. But the machine kept the card, which was then mailed back to the customer. This and other automated tellers were mainly experimental until the mid-seventies.

In 1974 the United States Supreme Court ruled that "help wanted" ads and other employment advertising could not specify gender. For example, a construction company could not publish an ad for a male worker, nor could an office specify it was looking for a female secretary. This ruling eliminated most of the blatant sexism in employment advertising and paved the way toward the end of age discrimination in hiring.

of exports for the first time since 1893. The steel and auto industries were especially hard hit. In the 1950s the United States had provided more than half of the world's steel; by 1978 the percentage had fallen to 16 percent. During the 1970s foreign automakers' share of the U.S. market rose from 17 to 37 percent.

In this economic climate, many businesses—especially those making cars, steel, textiles, and shoes—were forced to lay off workers, shut down factories, or even go out of business completely. Workers were also dislocated for other reasons. High taxes and other costs in the Northeast and in major cities led many businesses to move south to "Sun Belt" states. As a result, the nation's industrial centers began to decline, and inner cities continued to decay.

Transportation

STILL MORE SPEED

The full flowering of the air age in the 1960s added a new dimension to American mobility. It made practical the far-flung operations of multinational corporations and made possible Henry Kissinger's "shuttle diplomacy" during the Middle Eastern crises of 1973.

Air Travel

During the 1960s, Americans developed a national fancy for flying —a few select adventurers in spacecraft and travelers by the millions in jet aircraft. The conversion of the nation's commercial aircraft fleet to jet-powered aircraft started in 1960 and was nearly complete by the end of the decade. The new aircraft flew farther and faster and

► By 1970 the jumbo jet era was in full swing. Four 707s and three 747s park outside one of many terminals at the sprawling John F. Kennedy International Airport, one of the world's busiest airports.

could carry more passengers than similar aircraft powered by piston engines. For example, the Boeing 707, the nation's first commercial passenger jet, seated 179 and cruised at an average speed of 550 miles per hour.

By mid-decade, jet travel became almost commonplace. In 1966, for example, more than 3 million Americans traveled to Europe, some by ship, but most by jetliner. This surge in air travel caused a crisis in the nation's transportation system. Too many planes were trying to take off and land at too few airports. By 1968 a wait of two and a half hours in a holding pattern before landing was not uncommon.

The world's biggest airliner, Boeing's 747 jumbo jet, carried passengers for the first time in 1969, the year of the Apollo moon landing. The 747 was a 360-seat, 600-mile-per-hour giant of an airplane; its landing gear alone weighed 11 tons. The same year, a British-French joint venture produced the world's fastest passenger jet, the Concorde. Although staggeringly expensive to operate,

the elegant, needle-nosed craft could carry 100 passengers at a speed of more than 1,300 miles per hour. At that speed, it could cross the Atlantic in just about three hours. Wealthy American members of the "jet set" could streak to London or Paris for dinner and return the same day.

High-Speed Trains

High-speed travel was not limited to those who took to the air. In the mid-1960s the United States began to follow the Japanese lead in designing high-speed passenger trains. Gas-turbine-powered "turbotrains" reached 100 miles per hour on the New York–to–Boston run. High-speed electric trains, used on the New York–to–Washington route, averaged almost 80 miles per hour, 20 miles per hour faster than standard trains.

High speed did not ensure high profits, however. Most commercial passenger rail lines were out of business by the late 1960s. A publicly owned national rail service, called Amtrak, was formed from the defunct passenger railways and began service in 1971.

BART OPENS

In 1972 San Francisco opened the first sections of its new subway system, the Bay Area Rapid Transit (BART). It was the first subway built in America since World War II and the first in the world to be completely automated.

During the 1960s concerns about pollution, energy consumption, and traffic led to renewed interest in urban mass transportation in America. The effects of the automobile age had diminished or eliminated rapid transit systems in many cities, including San Francisco, in the 1940s and 1950s. Replacing these systems seemed a necessary—although costly—task.

SCIENCE AND TECHNOLOGY

In 1961, President Kennedy promised that Americans would walk on the moon by the end of the decade. Eight years later, the astronauts of Apollo 11 did just that—an event that both demonstrated and symbolized the ability of modern science and technology to change science fiction into reality. And earthbound changes were brought about as well. Between 1964 and 1975, science celebrated dramatic new achievements. Meanwhile, advances in technology profoundly changed the lifestyle of the American people.

America's love affair with modern advances cooled, however, as people began to realize that technology had its costs and limitations as well as its benefits. The biologist Barry Commoner, in presenting the basic principles of the budding ecology movement, put it this way: "1) Everything is connected to everything else; 2) everything must go somewhere; 3) nature knows best; and 4) there is no such thing as a free lunch—every gain is won at some cost."

Advances in technology brought with them a sharp rise in the pollution of the air, water, and soil, and a rapid depletion of nonrenewable resources, including coal, oil, and natural gas. By the mid-1970s, the issue had become acute. Would science and technology be able to solve the problems their advances had caused?

AT A GLANCE

▶ The New Frontier

▶ What About the Earth?

▶ Medical Revolution

▶ The Computer Age

▶ Solving Scientific Mysteries

DATAFILE

Science

Life expectancy at birth (yr.)	1964	1975
Males	66.9	68.8
Females	73.7	76.6

Top five causes of death, 1964–1975
1. Heart disease 2. Cancer 3. Accidents (all types)
4. Pneumonia and influenza 5. Diabetes mellitus

Technology

Miles of paved roads
1964 .... 2.8 mil.   1975 .... 3.1 mil.

Passenger miles traveled, 1975
Rail .... 10 bil.   Air .... 148 bil.

Households in 1975 with . . .
Electricity .... 100%   Indoor plumbing 97%
Telephone .... 90%   Television 97%

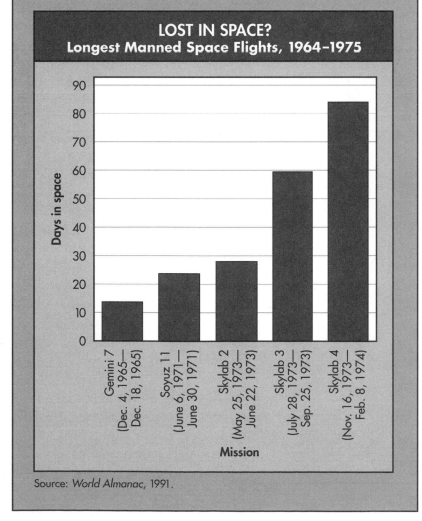

LOST IN SPACE?
Longest Manned Space Flights, 1964–1975

Y-axis: Days in space (0 to 90)
X-axis: Mission

- Gemini 7 (Dec. 4, 1965—Dec. 18, 1965)
- Soyuz 11 (June 6, 1971—June 30, 1971)
- Skylab 2 (May 25, 1973—June 22, 1973)
- Skylab 3 (July 28, 1973—Sep. 25, 1973)
- Skylab 4 (Nov. 16, 1973—Feb. 8, 1974)

Source: *World Almanac,* 1991.

THE NEW FRONTIER

On May 25, 1961, just six weeks after Soviet cosmonaut Yury Gagarin became the first person to travel in space, President John F. Kennedy made a dramatic announcement: "I believe that this nation should commit itself to achieving the goal, before the decade is out, of landing a man on the moon and returning him safely to earth." He continued, "No single space project in this period will be more impressive to mankind, or more important for the long-range exploration of space; and none will be so difficult or expensive to accomplish."

The quest for a moon landing proved enormously expensive and difficult, as Kennedy predicted. The effort involved 16 aerospace firms, 12,000 subcontractors, and scientists and engineers at 100 universities—a total of 400,000 people. The cost was equally staggering: more than $22 billion. But Kennedy was right on another count, too. When Neil Armstrong stepped onto the lunar surface on July 20, 1969, he made a momentous step in human history. It was, in Armstrong's words, a "giant leap for mankind."

From Mercury to Gemini

On May 5, 1961, Alan Shepard Jr. rose from Florida's Cape Canaveral in a cramped Mercury capsule atop a thundering Redstone rocket, bound for space and worldwide fame. The first American in space remained aloft for 15 minutes, a feat exceeded nine months later when John Glenn Jr. became the first American to orbit the earth. Glenn's 3,700-pound Mercury capsule, named *Friendship 7*, circled the earth three times after being thrust into orbit by a powerful Atlas rocket.

The series of one-man Mercury flights ended with the 34.5-hour, 22-orbit flight of Gordon Cooper Jr. in May 1963. By then, the Mercury astronauts had proven they could endure the tremendous force of acceleration and function in the weightless environment of space. Also, they were proving that they could compete with the Soviets.

The second phase of the space program began on March 23, 1965,

when Virgil "Gus" Grissom and John Young embarked on the first of 10 two-man Gemini missions. The Gemini program achieved one remarkable goal after another. *Gemini 1* was the first spacecraft to change its orbit while in space.

Edward White II, aboard *Gemini 4*, was the first American to "walk" in space—on June 3, 1965. White left the orbiting spacecraft, connected to it by only an "umbilical cord." He maneuvered for 20 minutes with the help of a hand-held air gun.

Gordon Cooper Jr. and Charles Conrad Jr., the crew of *Gemini 5*, made 120 earth orbits in eight days, showing that humans could remain in space long enough to complete a lunar mission. In December 1965, *Gemini 6* and *7* achieved the first rendezvous in space. At one point during this prearranged, controlled meeting, the two spacecraft were only 1 foot apart.

At the same time, unmanned spacecraft were busy gathering data about the moon. A series of Ranger probes sent back television pictures as they hurtled toward planned crash landings on the moon. In 1966, *Surveyor 1* made a soft lunar landing in an area of the moon called the "Ocean of Storms." It then sent back more than 10,000 television pictures of the moon's surface.

The Apollo Program

The three-man Apollo spacecraft dwarfed previous capsules in both size and technology. Each Apollo craft consisted of three parts: a service module, housing the engine that propelled the capsule out of

Major Satellite Launches, 1964–1975

Date launched	Name	Description
April 6, 1965	Early Bird	First commercial communications satellite
Jan. 11, 1967	Intelsat 2B	First of a series of satellites in stationary orbit; used for voice, data, and television communications
Sept. 7, 1967	Biosatellite 2	Took living cells, plants, and animals into space and brought them back to earth for study
Dec. 7, 1968	OAO-2	First orbiting astronomical observatory
Jan. 26, 1971	Intelsat 4A	First high-capacity international communications satellite
July 23, 1972	Landsat 1	Photographed the earth to provide information about the earth's natural resources
Nov. 9, 1972	Anik I	First Canadian communications satellite
June 10, 1973	Explorer 49	Conducted radio-astronomy research on the far side of the moon
May 17, 1974	SMS-1	First full-time weather satellite in synchronous orbit
May 30, 1974	ATS-6	Made two-way voice and picture communication possible in remote areas
Oct. 16, 1975	GOES-1	First weather satellite with enough speed to maintain a constant position over the earth

earth orbit to the moon and back; the command module, a sophisticated control center and the astronauts' home in space; and the lunar module, a buglike, foil-covered craft in which the astronauts descended to the moon's surface.

The Apollo capsule was launched into earth orbit by a three-stage Saturn 5 rocket, a complex cylinder of brute force that alone stood almost 300 feet tall. During the first 150 seconds of flight, the Saturn 5's J-2 first-stage engines developed 7.6 million pounds of thrust, burned half a million gallons of fuel, and accelerated the rocket to 6,100 miles per hour.

Three weeks before the scheduled February 1967 launch of *Apollo 1*, tragedy struck the moon-shot program. During preflight practice, the crew of *Apollo 1*—Gus Grissom, Edward White, and Roger Chaffee—were killed by a fire in their sealed capsule. Project Apollo was immediately halted until a safer capsule could be designed. By the fall of 1968, however, the Apollo program was going forward

again. From October 1968 to May 1969, a series of four space flights brought the Apollo astronauts to within 9 miles of the lunar surface. All systems were "go" to reach the moon.

A million spectators at Cape Kennedy cheered for the entire nation as Neil Armstrong, Edwin "Buzz" Aldrin Jr., and Michael Collins roared into the sky aboard *Apollo 11* on July 16, 1969. On July 20, Armstrong and Aldrin climbed aboard the lunar module, called the *Eagle*, and began their descent to the moon. At 4:17 P.M. EDT, Mission Control in Houston, Texas, received Armstrong's radio message: "Houston, Tranquility Base here. The *Eagle* has landed."

About six hours later, Armstrong climbed down the ladder and set foot on the moon. "That's one small step for man," he told a spellbound worldwide television audience, "one giant leap for mankind." In what President Nixon called "the greatest week in the history of the world since creation," America had achieved Kennedy's goal.

▲ Astronaut Edward White II (in photo at left) uses a hand-held propulsion device to maneuver back to his spacecraft after his "walk" in space. White (in the center of the photo above), along with Gus Grissom (left) and Roger Chaffee (right), was killed when fire engulfed the *Apollo 1* spacecraft.

NEW YORK BRIDGE LARGEST IN WORLD

The Verrazano-Narrows Bridge, which connects the New York City boroughs of Brooklyn and Staten Island, opened in 1964. It was the world's largest suspension bridge until the opening of the British Humber River Bridge in 1981.

The Verrazano-Narrows Bridge has steel support towers 680 feet high and a main span over 4,000 feet long. Its double-deck roadway has a total of 12 lanes. The four main support cables are 3 feet in diameter, and each cable contains over 142,000 miles of wire— over half the distance to the moon!

America's First Astronauts Conquer Space

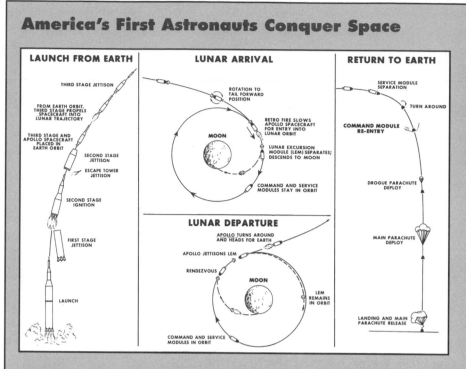

LAUNCH FROM EARTH

THIRD STAGE JETTISON

FROM EARTH ORBIT, THIRD STAGE PROPELS SPACECRAFT INTO LUNAR TRAJECTORY

THIRD STAGE AND APOLLO SPACECRAFT PLACED IN EARTH ORBIT

SECOND STAGE JETTISON

ESCAPE TOWER JETTISON

SECOND STAGE IGNITION

FIRST STAGE JETTISON

LAUNCH

LUNAR ARRIVAL

ROTATION TO TAIL FORWARD POSITION

RETRO FIRE SLOWS APOLLO SPACECRAFT FOR ENTRY INTO LUNAR ORBIT

MOON

LUNAR EXCURSION MODULE (LEM) SEPARATES; DESCENDS TO MOON

COMMAND AND SERVICE MODULES STAY IN ORBIT

LUNAR DEPARTURE

APOLLO TURNS AROUND AND HEADS FOR EARTH

APOLLO JETTISONS LEM

RENDEZVOUS

MOON

LEM REMAINS IN ORBIT

COMMAND AND SERVICE MODULES IN ORBIT

RETURN TO EARTH

SERVICE MODULE SEPARATION

TURN AROUND

COMMAND MODULE RE-ENTRY

DROGUE PARACHUTE DEPLOY

MAIN PARACHUTE DEPLOY

LANDING AND MAIN PARACHUTE RELEASE

◄ This diagram charts the course taken by the Apollo astronauts as they traveled to the moon and returned to earth. The two drawings in the center show how the lunar excursion module (LEM), used to transport two astronauts to the surface of the moon, separated from and returned to the command module. A third astronaut remained in the command module waiting to rendezvous with the LEM after the completion of work on the moon.

It was an exquisite moment of unparalleled wonder when, for the first time, a man—an earthling!—stood on the surface of the moon and commented nonchalantly, "The surface is fine and powdery. . . . I can pick it up loosely with my toe." Who was this suited superman, the cosmic cowboy who had conquered the dark mysteries of space travel astride his thundering space horse?

He was the astronaut Neil Armstrong, one of those chosen by the U.S. National Aeronautics and Space Administration (NASA) for manned space flights. He was one of a select group of men who had to meet the stringent criteria set by NASA. In the 1960s, candidates for astronaut training had to be younger than 40, shorter than 5 feet 11 inches, and in excellent physical condition; have a bachelor's degree or the equivalent; be a graduate of test pilot school; have at least 1,500 hours of total flying time; and be a qualified jet pilot. The lure of space attracted many of the best test pilots.

Capturing the imagination of a nation buffeted by the social and political turmoil of the 1960s, the astronauts became the heroes of the space age. They had the courage "to boldly go where no man has gone before," as stated in the television series *Star Trek*. They conquered space at a time when the American military endured defeat in Vietnam. They flawlessly controlled the complex Apollo rocket system in an age when the nation's economic machinery seemed beyond control.

In the eyes of many Americans, these men were short-haired, clean-cut symbols of diligence and responsibility for a nation whose long-haired, rebellious youth defied every rule and trusted no one over 30.

They were often portrayed as the best of men in what some considered the worst of times. As Michael Collins, pilot of the *Apollo 11* command module, put it, "Beyond the technological success of Apollo, it was certainly a victory for the human spirit, if your spirit is one that values exploration. Mankind's most complex expedition brought back to earth not only moon rocks but a renewed sense of confidence in the ability of the United States to succeed at whatever it deemed to be in its national interest."

Five more Apollo flights followed, with *Apollo 17* making the final visit to the moon in December 1972. Three years later, the astronauts of *Apollo 18* carried **détente** into space. The U.S. spacecraft docked, or joined, with the Soviet *Soyuz 19* to perform experiments and demonstrate the possibility of space rescue.

Planetary Explorations

The moon was not the only body in space that attracted serious exploration. A series of unmanned Mariner probes from 1962 to 1972 gave scientists dramatic close-up views of Mars, Venus, and Mercury. The Pioneer missions to Jupiter in the 1970s revealed clues about the development and composition of the solar system. Other triumphs occurred closer to home. In the *Skylab* space station, launched in 1973, nine astronauts spent more than 3,000 hours in orbit. There, they researched the long-term effects of living in space.

WHAT ABOUT THE EARTH?

In 1962 the National Academy of Sciences made a report on the nation's resources to President Kennedy. The Academy recommended that the United States shift away from a policy of conserving scarce resources and pursue the "wise management of plenty." That attitude suited most Americans. They believed that their standard of living, already five times higher than the world's average,

◄ In July 1975, a historic moment occurred when the U.S. spacecraft *Apollo 18* linked up in space with the Soviet craft *Soyuz 19*. American astronaut Thomas P. Stafford (left) meets Soviet cosmonaut Alexei A. Leonov in the tunnel of the Apollo docking module after the two ships were locked together.

would continue to improve. If the nation ran out of coal or copper, modern technology would undoubtedly invent a better and probably cheaper substitute.

This belief in an unlimited supply of resources and the unbounded power of technology was widespread during the early 1960s. Resources seemed plentiful, and the space program was amazing even its most optimistic supporters. No problem seemed too large for "can do" Americans to fix.

Slowly, however, people began to realize that modern technology had its dark side as well. For example, the nation's demand for electricity had doubled every ten years since Thomas Edison perfected the light bulb in 1879. One November evening in 1965, a power surge raced through a small relay in a hydroelectric station near Niagara Falls, Canada. The relay, which was not built for such high power demands, failed. This failure caused a chain reaction

EARLY BIRD SATELLITE LAUNCHED

Intelsat 1, also called *Early Bird*, was launched into orbit on April 6, 1965, from Cape Kennedy, Florida. A product of a multinational group, this 85-pound communications satellite ushered in a new era in worldwide commercial communications. The group's member nations jointly own the Intelsat system of satellites.

Early Bird was a highly successful commercial venture, providing customers with international communications services. However, the capabilities of the satellite were somewhat limited. *Early Bird,* which was retired in August 1969, could carry only 240 telephone circuits or one television channel.

The multinational organization has developed more sophisticated generations of satellites since *Early Bird*. *Intelsat 6*, for instance, can carry at least 33,000 simultaneous telephone calls plus four television channels.

TECHNOLOGICAL
HIGHLIGHTS, 1964–1975
compact microwave, 1967
safety caps on dangerous
    products, such as turpentine,
    1970
pocket calculator, 1972
disposable razor, 1975
computerized supermarket
    checkout, 1975

that left 30 million people in the United States and Canada without power. Modern civilization came to a halt: trains and elevators stopped, computers "crashed," factories shut down, freezers thawed, prisoners rioted, televisions went blank, and stores were looted. The Great Northeast Blackout of 1965 illustrated what the *New York Times* called "the prison of modern technology."

Was the answer to build more power plants? **Fossil fuel**–powered generating stations had already fouled the nation's air and water; Lake Erie had been pronounced dead from pollution. Nuclear power had not lived up to the promise of providing cheap electricity. And on October 5, 1966, the nuclear reactor at an electricity-generating station on Lake Erie malfunctioned. This accident caused people to worry about the dangers of nuclear power, including cancer-causing radiation.

Environmental crises mounted. DDT and other pesticides, along with chemical fertilizers and herbicides, had entered the **food chain** and threatened both human and animal life. Also, public concern grew over the use of cancer-causing substances in food processing.

The dependence of America on petroleum exacted a terrible price not only on air quality but also on the seas. In 1967, the jumbo oil tanker *Torrey Canyon*, owned by an American company, struck a reef off the coast of England and spilled 118,000 tons of oil into the English Channel. Two years later, a drilling rig near the California coast collapsed, spilling 231,000 barrels of oil and fouling 40 miles of beaches.

Awareness Increases

The moon landing in 1969 marked a turning point for many people. They began to wonder if technology had done as much as it could for people who remained on earth, with its polluted air and water, mounting heaps of solid waste, and rapidly dwindling resources. If we can put a man on the moon, they said, why can't we solve our problems here on earth?

The first Earth Day, held in April 1970, marked the climax of the early struggles to stop pollution. On this day, environmentalists and ecologists sponsored nationwide demonstrations to teach people about problems with the environment. Some people wore gas

Torrey Canyon Fouls Waters and Beaches

The oil spill that took place in 1967 off the southwest coast of England was one of the first to gain widespread international attention. On March 18, the U.S. oil tanker *Torrey Canyon* was grounded at Land's End, England. The tanker lost 118,000 tons of oil—over 33 million gallons.

The oil polluted both French and English beaches for several hundred miles and killed waterfowl and other marine life. Television coverage in Europe and the United States displayed the effects of the spill to a horrified public.

The 1967 spill, along with the 1969 explosion of an oil rig off the coast of Santa Barbara, California, prompted concerned citizens to form environmental groups. These groups made the public aware of the need to improve spill cleanup methods. They also worked to encourage companies to take preventive measures against such accidents.

masks to protest air pollution. Others returned trash to the companies that produced it. Wisconsin senator Gaylord Nelson warned, "Progress—American style—adds up each year to 200 million tons of smoke and fumes, 7 million junked cars, 20 million tons of paper, 48 billion cans, and 28 billion bottles."

The nation's perspective on progress was slowly changing. In 1971, for example, the U.S. Senate debated a complete ban on the sale and use of DDT. That same year, the Senate voted not to continue funding the development of the costly supersonic transport (SST) project—a project some thought would cause noise and air pollution. Federal and state government agencies spearheaded intensive efforts to clean up rivers and restock them with fish. And in 1975, Oregon became the first state to ban **chlorofluorocarbons,** gases that were contaminating the atmos-

phere. These actions alone did not solve the environmental problem. However, they did show that Americans were serious about protecting the fragile web of life that "progress" had put at risk.

Medicine

MEDICAL REVOLUTION

The stunning success of the Apollo space program dazzled the world with the prowess of science and modern technology during the 1960s and early 1970s. But space was not the only technological frontier of the period. In December 1967, Dr. Christiaan Barnard led a 30-person team of South African surgeons, physicians, and nurses in performing a dramatic and innovative procedure: the world's first successful heart transplant.

AMERICAN NOBEL PRIZE WINNERS, 1964–1975

Chemistry
Robert B. Woodward, 1965
Robert S. Mulliken, 1966
Lars Onsager, 1968
Christian B. Anfinsen, Stanford Moore, and William H. Stein, 1972
Paul J. Flory, 1974

Physiology or Medicine
Konrad E. Bloch, 1964
Charles B. Huggins and Francis Peyton Rous, 1966
Haldan Keffer Hartline and George Wald, 1967
Robert W. Holley, Har Gobind Khorana, and Marshall W. Nirenberg, 1968
Max Delbrück, Alfred D. Hershey, and Salvador Luria, 1969
Julius Axelrod, 1970
Earl W. Sutherland Jr., 1971
Gerald M. Edelman, 1972
Albert Claude and George Emil Palade, 1974
David Baltimore, Howard Temin, and Renato Dulbecco, 1975

▶ The South African physician Dr. Christiaan Barnard conducted the first successful heart transplant in Groote Schuur Hospital in Cape Town in December 1967.

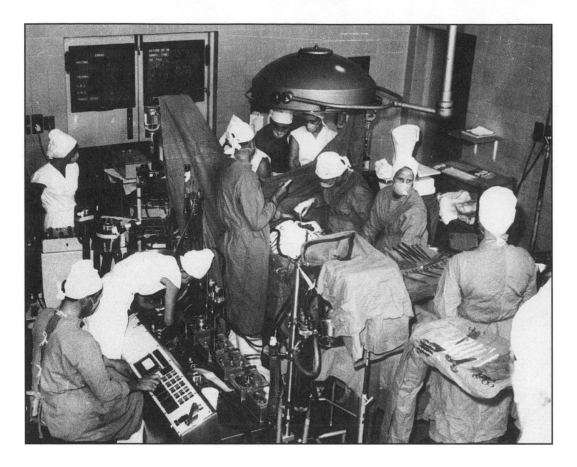

Physics

Richard P. Feynman and Julian S. Schwinger, 1965

Hans A. Bethe, 1967

Luis W. Alvarez, 1968

Murray Gell-Mann, 1969

John Bardeen, Leon N. Cooper, and John R. Schrieffer, 1972

Ivar Giaever, 1973

James Rainwater and Ben Mottelson, 1975

Dr. Barnard's patient, Louis Washkansky, died 18 days later from lung complications, but medical history had been made during the five-hour operation. The stage was set for a series of similar operations in the years that followed.

Dr. Barnard's casual comment during a heart transplant operation early in 1968 revealed the magnitude of medicine's progress. "We are not going into the unknown," he remarked. "We are going where we have been before." Within one year of the first transplant, 95 human hearts had been taken from donors who had just died and implanted in the chests of critically ill patients with failing hearts. With these remarkable advances, however, came troubling new questions. Who would pay the staggering cost of heart transplant surgery? How would scarce donor hearts be allocated to waiting transplant candidates? Balanced against these serious issues was the hope that transplants would not be needed at all someday.

After all, transplants were not the only new way to treat heart disease. A clinic in Cleveland, Ohio, developed the coronary bypass operation at about the same time Dr. Barnard performed the first transplant. The same year, a new study linked lower blood cholesterol levels with a reduced risk of developing heart disease. In 1970, French surgeons implanted the first nuclear-powered heart pacemaker. These treatment options gave physicians and their patients new hope in their fight against America's number-one killer.

Other medical advances crowded the scientific horizon. In 1968, researchers developed a technique called "amniocentesis." In this procedure, a sample of amniotic fluid from the womb is examined in order to detect fetal genetic disorders early in pregnancy. This process gave pregnant women the option of aborting fetuses affected by crippling diseases such as Down syndrome and muscular dystrophy. For women unable to conceive children, the news from

The Cigarette Saga

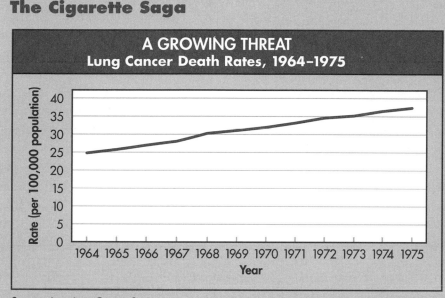

A GROWING THREAT
Lung Cancer Death Rates, 1964–1975

Source: American Cancer Society.

▲ Cigarette smoking is the leading cause of lung cancer. The risk that a person will get lung cancer starts to lessen as soon as he or she stops smoking.

Ever since tobacco companies publicized the health benefits of cigarette smoking in the 1920s, medical researchers have suspected otherwise. By 1950, large-scale studies had demonstrated that smoking had precisely the opposite effect from that claimed by the companies: people who developed lung cancer smoked more heavily than those who did not develop lung cancer. The evidence was so overwhelming that in 1964 the U.S. Public Health Service issued a Surgeon General's Report on Smoking and Health. The report warned that cigarette smoking increases the risk of lung cancer. Smoking was also linked to heart disease, emphysema, and chronic bronchitis.

The facts seemed irrefutable. For example, a study published in 1966 revealed that eight times as many male smokers aged 45 to 64 died of lung cancer as men who never smoked regularly. Yet the tobacco industry insisted that smoking had not been proven to cause cancer. At the same time, tobacco companies introduced cigarettes with lower tar and nicotine content. The surgeon general did not feel that these changes minimized smoking's harmful effects, however.

Despite the tobacco industry's denials and so-called safer products, the message about cancer's deadly effects began to have an impact. As of 1970, about 60 percent of all smokers in the United States had tried to stop smoking; a third succeeded for a significant period of time. Federal law also reflected the concern over the effects of smoking. In 1965, all packs of cigarettes were required to carry this warning: "Caution: Cigarette smoking may be hazardous to your health." In 1970, cigarette commercials were banned from television and radio. Eventually, stronger warnings were added to cigarette packs, and smoking was banned in a number of public places.

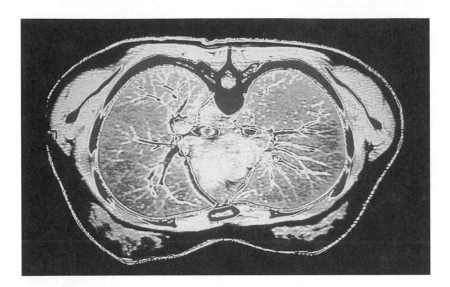

▲ This CAT scan shows a cross section of a patient's heart and lungs. The image, created by the combined use of a computer and X-rays, produces a clearer picture and greater detail than that provided by X-rays alone.

Cambridge, England, in 1969 was especially encouraging. Doctors there succeeded in fertilizing a human egg outside the mother's body. They then implanted the egg in the mother's womb so she could carry it to full development.

Medical researchers also achieved gains in the prevention and diagnosis of disease. In 1969, a vaccine for rubella, often called "German measles," became available for the first time. Three years later, thanks to insights from physicists and engineers, computerized axial tomography (CAT) scan equipment entered the market. This safe, painless diagnostic equipment revolutionized medicine by providing detailed, accurate information about internal organs.

Technology

THE COMPUTER AGE

Between 1964 and 1975, the impact of computers and computer-driven technology was revolutionary. Only 4,000 computers existed worldwide in 1961. By the mid-1970s, the number had multiplied to more than 100,000. Computers kept business records, wrote music, evaluated marketing statistics, conducted scientific experiments, designed new products, simulated complex economic events, and controlled the flow of highway traffic.

The successful lunar landing by *Apollo 11* in 1969 would have been impossible without extensive use of computers to control propulsion, communication, and navigational systems. A computer in the Apollo command module, for example, stored the coordinates of 37 stars. To determine the precise position of the spacecraft, an astronaut aligned the cross hairs of a computer-linked sextant on one of the stars and told the computer which star it was. The computer took over from there.

From Power to Productivity

The computer revolution of the 1960s was made possible by the invention of the integrated circuit, a tiny chip of silicon that contained a series of linked electronic circuits. First produced by Texas Instruments in 1959, the circuits dramatically reduced both the size of computers and the power needed to operate them. In the space occupied by one circuit in 1960, 100 circuits could fit in 1964; by 1975, 10,000 could fit in the same space. Digital Equipment Corporation used this new technology to produce the first small, efficient, and relatively inexpensive minicomputer in 1963.

At the same time, IBM and Sperry-Rand raced feverishly to

develop the fastest possible super-computer with the greatest processor capacity. But the demand for these very large, powerful, and expensive machines was limited to a few customers. So in 1964 IBM introduced its System/360, which featured a wide range of central processors, storage devices, printers, and other peripherals. All were fully compatible with each other, and customers could tailor their systems to meet individual needs and budgets. The System/360 was very successful, with 1,000 orders a month pouring in. The true computer revolution had begun.

By the 1970s, most computer manufacturers and their customers recognized that the key to a computer's productivity was not, in most cases, the raw speed of its central processor. Rather, productivity was determined by how skillfully the computer's **software** applied the computer's processor capacity to specific needs. As a result, an entirely new industry developed within the computer field to write software programs. Word processing, spreadsheet, and database programs soon became as familiar as central processing units (CPUs) and printers to the nation's growing number of computer users.

Personal Computers
In 1971 an engineer at the Intel Corporation invented the **microprocessor.** This "computer on a chip" represented a great advance in processor technology. Computer designers could place dozens of integrated circuits on a single silicon chip. Personal computers—inexpensive machines that fit on a

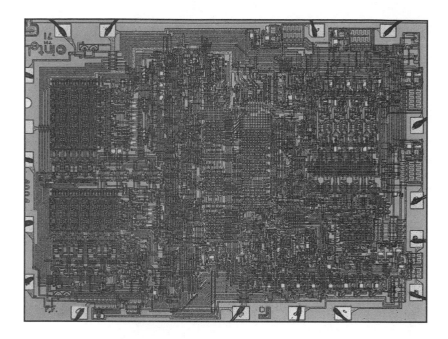

desktop—based on an Intel microprocessor soon followed. The first, called the Altair 8800, appeared in 1975 as a $399 kit for do-it-yourself electronics buffs. Apple, Kaypro, Morrow, and other companies were quick to tap the growing market for affordable yet powerful personal computers.

A 1977 article in *Scientific American* magazine compared the first personal computers to the 30-ton ENIAC, unveiled in 1946. "Today's microcomputer, at a cost of perhaps $300, has more computer capacity than the first large electronic computer, ENIAC," the author wrote. "It is twenty times faster, has a larger memory, is thousands of times more reliable, consumes the power of a light bulb rather than that of a locomotive, occupies 1/30,000 the volume and costs 1/10,000 as much." Within ten years of the introduction of the personal computer in the United States, over 25 million units were humming in homes, schools, businesses, and government offices.

▲ This silicon chip, only ¼ inch wide, is the microprocessor of a microcomputer. Invented by Ted Hoff of Intel Corporation in 1971, the chip contains the electronic circuits that enable the computer to perform its functions.

"By continuously embracing technologies we relate ourselves to them. . . . That is why we must, to use them at all, serve these objects as gods or minor religions."
—Marshall McLuhan, 1964

Technological Advances Change Entertainment

The late 1960s and early 1970s gave birth to many new developments in communications and entertainment technology that would affect American life in the decades to come.

In 1967 R. M. Dolby developed a system for eliminating background hiss on audio recordings. RCA contributed to audio technology with the development of the compact disk in 1972. Visual electronics were advanced when Sony Corporation of Japan invented the videocassette in 1969. Philips Corporation, a Dutch company, followed with the invention of the video disk in 1972. Pong, the first video game, was also released in 1972.

Although it took several years for these products to be perfected and made easily available to consumers, by the late 1970s and early 1980s they had changed the way Americans spent their leisure time.

Science

SOLVING SCIENTIFIC MYSTERIES

Describing a rock has always been easier than describing a mouse or a horse, not to mention a human being; rocks don't run through mazes, flee when threatened, or—most significantly—have babies. Scientists have long been puzzled by living things. What single set of characteristics unites them and, at the same time, distinguishes them from all nonliving things? How are the unique characteristics of one

generation transmitted to successive generations?

Breakthroughs in Science

The first breakthrough came in 1953, when the scientists Francis Crick and James D. Watson discovered the structure of DNA, the complex molecules used by all life on earth to store and transmit genetic information. Between 1961 and 1966, the scientists Har Gobind Khorana, Marshall W. Nirenberg, and Robert W. Holley deciphered the DNA code. All five scientists received the Nobel Prize for physiology or medicine for their work. In time, researchers were able to specify precisely how various forms of life differ. The sequence of amino acids in a certain DNA-controlled protein molecule, for example, differs at 4 points in a pig and a rabbit and at 47 points in a pig and a cauliflower.

By 1970, Khorana had successfully synthesized a DNA gene, the basic unit of heredity. This historic achievement made **genetic engineering**—human manipulation of the genetic code—seem a realistic possibility. Would scientists someday rewrite the "recipe" for human beings and other forms of life?

Research ventures in other fields promised more scientific advances. The first laser, built by the American scientist Theodore H. Maiman, was operated in 1960. However, the full potential of its intensely powerful beam of light for communications was not immediately apparent. In 1968, though, a laser beam sent from Kitt Peak National Observatory in Arizona was recorded by a television camera aboard *Surveyor 7. Surveyor 7* was

NEW WORDS

printout

cable TV

interface

time frame

nuke

an unmanned spacecraft located on the surface of the moon—more than 200,000 miles from the earth. Since in theory all the world's radio, television, and telephone messages could be carried by a single laser beam, the possibilities for laser-based communications were unlimited.

Scientists also probed the heavens far beyond the moon. In 1967, astronomers in Britain detected rapid pulsations coming from four locations in space. "Our first thought," one astronomer said, "was that this was another intelligence trying to contact us." They finally decided that the "pulsars" were the natural vibrations of dying stars. Astronomers also discovered two new galaxies in 1971.

Life under the sea received equal time during the 1960s and early 1970s. Efforts were spurred on by President Kennedy, who said, "Knowledge of the oceans is more than a matter of curiosity. Our very survival may hinge upon it." Using diving bells and deep-sea submarines, marine scientists surveyed the rugged terrain and studied the life forms at the bottom of the sea. There they discovered vast deposits of oil, gas, and mineral ores.

Scientists also set new records for living below the sea; ten men lived 30 days in *Sealab II* at a depth of 205 feet, and four lived 50 feet beneath the surface for 60 days in *Tektite*. The crew of *Tektite* also included five women aquanauts—a first.

Nagging Concerns

Even as scientists pushed back the boundaries of knowledge, however,

◀ Scott Carpenter (right), former astronaut, directed the Navy's Sealab program, a series of underwater-living experiments.

their discoveries created tough new questions. For example, should scientists use genetic engineering to change the basic structure of human genes? By 1974, many scientists were voicing concerns over such experimentation. The National Academy of Sciences called a halt to research in genetic engineering until safe techniques could be developed.

Science was also viewed as a potential threat in another way: many people feared that advances in science could trigger new technologies that could heighten the possibility of a nuclear disaster. In 1974, scientists and engineers in Great Britain, France, China, and India conducted tests of nuclear weapons. Now, many nations, not just the United States and the Soviet Union, had their fingers poised on nuclear buttons. The challenge of enjoying the benefits of science and technology while escaping its hazards became increasingly difficult in the years ahead.

EMERGING THEORY REVOLUTIONIZES EARTH SCIENCES

In the late 1960s, the theory of plate tectonics took hold in the scientific community. The theory states that the earth's surface is broken up into about 20 large sections, called "plates." The plates are about 60 miles thick and rest on a semiliquid base, called the "mantle."

According to geologists and other earth scientists, the continents began as a single mass that later broke up, with the continents subsequently drifting to their present positions. As plates shifted millions of years ago, mountains, trenches, and other physical features of the landscape were formed. Where the edges of plates meet and form fault lines, major earthquakes occur.

ARTS AND ENTERTAINMENT

Life in America between 1964 and 1975 was full and complex, filled with dramatic achievements, yet fraught with explosive tensions. The nation's best scientists conquered the dark mysteries of space, but its finest troops foundered in the murky jungles of Vietnam. Blacks and women made strides to overcome centuries of injustice but not without a profound social and legal struggle with those who opposed equality. America's economy faltered, many of its youth rebelled, and a president resigned in disgrace.

The arts and entertainment of the period reflected this restlessness, this passion and fragmentation. Yet traditional values shone through as well, sometimes opposing change, other times ignoring it completely. In other words, it was a period that embraced both the

AT A GLANCE

► **The Power of Popular Music**

► **Classical Music and Dance**

► **New Themes in Literature**

► **The Influence of Television**

► **Movies: From Innocence to Experience**

► **The Theater Continues to Entertain**

► **A New Look in Art**

romantic song "I Want to Hold Your Hand," by the Beatles (above, with Ed Sullivan), and the grim "Eve of Destruction," by Barry MacGuire. Jacqueline Susann's novel The Love Machine *shot to the top of the best-seller lists, but so did Joyce Carol Oates's satirical* Expensive People. The Andy Griffith Show *comforted television viewers with its family-style humor;* All in the Family, *on the other hand, used the family situation comedy to expose bigotry and prejudice.*

The music and art of the period were not consistent and unified, but then neither was America. Both tradition and rebellion existed side by side in the society and in the arts and entertainment of the time. Arts and entertainment provided both escape from and confrontation of the problems of the time.

DATAFILE

Attendance and sales	1964	1975
Movie attendance (weekly)	44 mil.	19 mil.
Reading material sales (excluding educational)	$4.7 bil.	$9.9 bil.
Home audio/visual expenditures	$6.4 bil.	$15.7 bil.

The press	1965	1975
Number of daily newspapers	1,751	1,775
Circulation	60.4 mil.	60.7 mil.
Number of magazines	8,990	9,657
Circulation	NA	NA

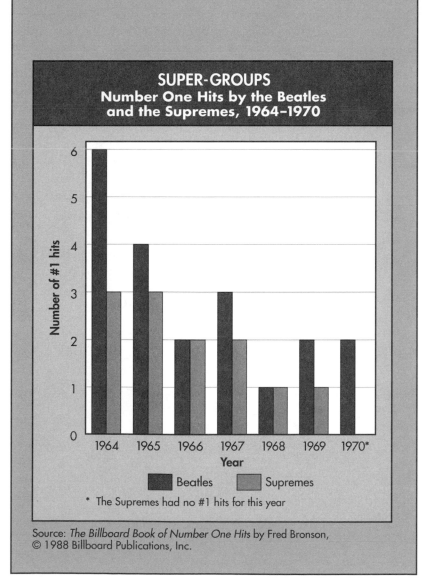

SUPER-GROUPS
Number One Hits by the Beatles and the Supremes, 1964–1970

(bar chart, y-axis: Number of #1 hits, x-axis: Year)

Beatles   Supremes

* The Supremes had no #1 hits for this year

Source: *The Billboard Book of Number One Hits* by Fred Bronson,
© 1988 Billboard Publications, Inc.

THE POWER OF POPULAR MUSIC

"You say you want a revolution? Well, you know, we all want to change the world." These words, opening lines of the Beatles' hit single "Revolution," show how much music changed in the 1960s. No longer merely entertainment, popular music became a powerful means of protest and an effective force for social change. Rock and roll was not the first form of music to sound a protest, of course; the blues had been doing that for decades and folk music for many years as well. But during the sixties, rock artists mined blues and folk traditions and fashioned from them the voice of an era.

The British "Invasion"
Popular music in the 1960s was greatly influenced by an "invasion" from across the sea. British rockers, attracted by the lucrative American music market, began to capture the hearts and pocketbooks of American teenagers and college students. Many groups came and performers gained instant fame, but most returned to obscurity just as quickly. The Beatles, however, followed by the Rolling Stones and The Who, left a lasting impression on an entire generation of American youth.

The Beatles, from the moment they first appeared on American television in February 1964, created "an explosion of joy at being young and alive," said one reviewer. Their songs—"All You Need Is Love," "We Can Work It Out," "I

The Fab Four from Liverpool

From the moment the Beatles appeared on Ed Sullivan's top-rated television variety show in 1964, their tuneful music and exuberant charm touched something deep and restless in young people across America. These four musicians from Liverpool, England—John Lennon, Paul McCartney, George Harrison, and Ringo Starr—were mobbed by adoring fans wherever they played.

Beatlemania was all-consuming: American teens copied the Beatles' clothes and mop-head hairstyles, memorized their jokes, and imitated their Liverpudlian slang. When the Beatles went on tour, their concerts were a frenzy of mass idol worship. "We were in the same place, breathing the same air, sharing the same moment with the Beatles themselves, and the ecstasy was indescribable," explained one concertgoer. Writing of the Beatles' 1965 performance at the Cow Palace in San Francisco, author Tom Wolfe noted, "The whole front section of the arena becomes a writhing, seething mass of little girls waving their arms in the air . . . like a single colonial animal with a thousand waving pink tentacles."

Between 1964 and 1970, the Beatles released 22 albums and dozens of singles, selling millions of records as well as countless Beatles T-shirts, motor scooters, lunch boxes, pillows, and sneakers. With their popularity ensured, the Beatles began to introduce some musical innovations. For instance, the group released *Sergeant Pepper's Lonely Hearts Club Band* in 1967, the first album that presented a theme rather than a group of unrelated songs. The Beatles also used instruments not normally associated with rock music. In their musical arrangements, many of which were written by Lennon and McCartney, they used classical violins and cellos as well as exotic instruments such as the sitar.

By 1970, however, the Magical Mystery Tour was over. The Beatles broke up. Millions of devout fans hoped and prayed that the Beatles would reunite, if only for just one more concert, but they never did. Throughout the 1970s, the four former Beatles each pursued their own music careers. When John Lennon was shot dead outside his New York City apartment building in 1980, the chance of a reunion also died.

◄ American fans scream with delight during a sold-out concert given by the Beatles at Shea Stadium in New York in August 1965.

Feel Fine," "Help," "Eleanor Rigby," "Yesterday"—captured the energy, desire, and frustration of exuberant, sold-out crowds across the country.

Unlike many other British rock groups, the Rolling Stones reflected on the darker side of human nature. *Time* magazine called the Stones "perverted, outrageous, violent, repulsive, ugly, incoherent, a travesty. That's what's good about them." Led by the surly vocals of Mick Jagger and the exciting blues guitar of Keith Richards, the Stones rocked through "Satisfaction," "Honky Tonk Woman," "Jumpin' Jack Flash," and "Let's Spend the Night Together." Their raucous concerts included songs denouncing racism, injustice, and the war in Vietnam.

The Who, one critic wrote, "were the most unsightly mob to emerge from the British Invasion. . . . Their sound was anarchy, chaos, pure noise—a definition of one kind of sixties rock." The lyrics of "My Gen-eration" set the tone: "People try to put us down / Just because we get around / Things they do look awful cold / Hope I die before I get old." Pete Townshend, the group's lead guitarist who routinely smashed his guitar onstage, said, "Rock won't eliminate your problems. But it will let you sort of dance all over them." One of The Who's albums was the rock opera *Tommy*, in which a single story is told through the album's individual songs.

Protests and Visions

Bob Dylan, folk-rock poet of the **counterculture,** has rightly been called the most influential songwriter of the 1960s. His intelligent lyrics made him enormously popular with disenchanted college students. Dylan's "Blowin' in the Wind" quickly became an anthem for the growing peace movement. His "Like a Rolling Stone" eloquently captured the sentiment of many young people: "How does it

POPULAR SONGS, 1964–1975

1964	"I Want to Hold Your Hand"
1965	"Mr. Tambourine Man"
1966	"The Sounds of Silence"
1967	"A Natural Woman"
1968	"Sunshine of Your Love"
1969	"Get Back"
1970	"I'll Be There"
1971	"Theme from *Shaft*"
1972	"Anticipation"
1973	"Rocky Mountain High"
1974	"Seasons in the Sun"
1975	"The Hustle"

▶ In their music, both Bob Dylan (left) and Joan Baez (right) expressed the disillusionment of young people of the sixties.

feel, how does it feel / To be without a home / Like a complete unknown / Like a rolling stone?"

Other musicians echoed the concerns of many young people of the time: Janis Joplin in her anguished blues-based "Ball and Chain"; the Doors in their invitation to "Light My Fire"; Simon and Garfunkel in their social lament "The Sounds of Silence"; Jimi Hendrix, Jefferson Airplane, and the Grateful Dead in their psychedelic, or acid, rock tunes; and folk-rocker Joan Baez in her songs of strident political activism. These popular musicians in the 1960s and 1970s used the sounds of rock and roll to promote a revolution—a celebration of love, peace, sex, and drugs in a society obsessed with war, conformity, and greed. In the long run, however, the revolution exacted its toll on those who pushed too hard at the boundaries. In 1970, for example, both Jimi Hendrix and Janis Joplin died of drug overdoses. The next year, Jim Morrison, lead singer of The Doors, died of a heart attack.

Soul, Pop, and Country

Rock and roll was not the only music of the sixties and early seventies. During this time, Berry Gordy's Motown Records featured soul artists who consistently topped the music charts: the Four Tops, the Temptations, Smokey Robinson and the Miracles, Diana Ross and the Supremes, Stevie Wonder, and Gladys Knight and the Pips. The Supremes, a female singing trio, had record sales second only to those of the Beatles during the 1960s. Some of the finest moments of sixties soul—a marriage of gospel and blues, of heaven and hell, according to Aretha Franklin—are captured in Franklin's "Respect" and James Brown's "Papa's Got a Brand New Bag."

Pop music, more mainstream and commercial than rock and roll, emerged in the folk ballads of Carole King, the surfing-lifestyle hits of the Beach Boys, and the 1970s sounds of the Carpenters, Three Dog Night, Olivia Newton-John, Sonny and Cher, Elton John, and Chicago. Country music, once a regional phenomenon, also began to stake its claim on the American music scene through performers such as Bobbie Gentry, Loretta Lynn, and Johnny Cash.

The Business of Music

With the huge success of the Beatles and other rock superstars, the music business mushroomed. The Beatles' sold-out world tour seemed to have a trickle-down effect: performers and bands that once played small club dates now performed concerts before large audiences. Both free music festivals and paid concerts drew thousands of fans anxious to see and hear their favorite artists. In the early 1970s, musicians performed at elaborately staged rock megashows, complete with lights, smoke machines, and complex stage sets.

CLASSICAL MUSIC AND DANCE

Even in the best of economic times, many classical orchestras and dance companies face an uncertain financial future. And the period from 1964 to 1975 was far from the best of times. Urban crises had forced many cities to cut arts funding. Federal **subsidies** were not available because the federal budget was awash in red ink as a result of the war. In 1969, for example, Atlanta closed its opera, and the Cincinnati and Indiana orchestras were merged. Those companies that survived often faced strikes from dissatisfied musicians.

Nevertheless, the orchestras, operas, and ballet companies of the

A "Happening" at Woodstock

For three days in August 1969, at least 400,000 people, most 15 to 25 years old, gathered at the Woodstock Music and Art Fair to share a unique experience. The festival, held on a 600-acre dairy farm in Bethel, New York, was remarkable for its music, its size, and the mood of the audience. At this free concert, where food, sanitation, and space were in short supply and where people had to sleep on the ground or in cars, the crowds remained peaceful and friendly. They enjoyed the music and each other's company.

Some of the best-known rock and blues performers appeared. Joan Baez, Arlo Guthrie, Jimi Hendrix, Jefferson Airplane, Janis Joplin, and The Who, among others, entertained. The performers were as impressed by the size and behavior of the audience as the crowds were thrilled by the stars' performances. The Woodstock event epitomized the free-spirited, fun-loving side of the youth of the sixties.

period continued to win high praise for their musical achievements, and some even opened new facilities. The new Metropolitan Opera House opened at Lincoln Center in New York City in 1966. Five years later, the John F. Kennedy Center for the Performing Arts opened in Washington, D.C., with the premiere of Leonard Bernstein's *Mass*.

As always, great artists lifted the spirits and stretched the imagination of the nation's music lovers. In 1965 the celebrated pianist Vladimir Horowitz returned to Carnegie Hall after a 12-year absence from the stage. The defection to the West of two Russian ballet dancers, arguably the two greatest male dancers of all time, bracket

Leonard Bernstein's Zest for Making Music

Leonard Bernstein was one of the most significant American composers and conductors of the twentieth century. Even as a child, "he was frighteningly gifted," recalled his piano teacher. "He could read, sing, and memorize anything. He absorbed in one lesson an arrangement that took most of my pupils five or six lessons to learn."

Most musicians choose one specialty: performing, conducting, or composing. Bernstein, however, excelled at all three. The *New York Times* magazine called him a "triple-note man of music."

From 1958 to 1969, Bernstein was musical director and conductor of the New York Philharmonic Orchestra, the first American to hold that post. He conducted opera in Paris, New York, and Vienna, and he composed several symphonies, ballets, and operas. He wrote music for several Broadway shows, including

West Side Story and *On the Town.* Bernstein also performed a series of television concerts especially for children, produced a number of hugely popular television talks on music, and wrote several books.

The title of Bernstein's first book tells the entire story of his long and varied career: *The Joy of Music.* Until he died in 1990, his greatest gift to his millions of fans around the world was his unrestrained enthusiasm for and sheer delight in making music. "Lenny," as he was affectionately known to his friends, had an insatiable appetite for life, which for him always involved music. For example, Bernstein loved to attend parties; almost always, he was the center of attention. "I just ran for the piano as soon as I got in the door and stayed there until they threw me out," he explained. "It was as though I didn't exist without music."

Late one night in 1929, the quietness of the Bernstein household in Massachusetts was disturbed by the sound of someone tinkering at the piano. The father, who was half asleep, stumbled into the living room and shouted, "Lenny, don't you know what time it is? It's two o'clock! What in heaven's name are you doing?" Eleven-year-old Lenny answered with conviction: "I have to do this. The sounds are in my head and I have to get them out."

the period: Rudolf Nureyev in 1961 and Mikhail Baryshnikov in 1974. Nureyev's breathtaking performance of *Romeo and Juliet* with Margot Fonteyn and London's Royal Ballet was even then recognized as the stuff of legend: the two leading dancers made 33 curtain calls.

Two very different musical trends marked the work of the period's classical musicians. One, the so-called early music movement, attempted to re-create the original effect of early classical music by using instruments and playing styles that the music's first performers would have used. The other sought to explore the interaction between classical music and modern technology.

Milton Babbitt, a musician and mathematician turned composer, wanted total control of all aspects of his musical compositions, leading him to experiment with electronic synthesizers. John Cage pushed the traditional boundaries of sound and structure even further. His compositions featured unorthodox sounds: cowbells, tin cans, banging doors, and electronic distortion. In one of his earlier pieces, *4´33˝*, the performer sits in front of a piano for 4 minutes and 33 seconds, playing nothing.

Literature

NEW THEMES IN LITERATURE

At 127 pages including pictures, it was not the longest book of the period, nor was it the biggest seller, though it sold more than 1 million copies in hardback. But Richard Bach's tale of a renegade seagull in his 1970 book *Jonathan Livingston Seagull* captured more than a few themes of the period. Bach spun an engaging yarn about a young seagull's quest to exceed conventional limits and break traditional boundaries, his search for new meaning and purpose, and his realization that self-fulfillment can come at a high cost. It was an adventure of discovery for Jonathan and the readers who cheered him on. "The only true law is that which leads to freedom," Jonathan said. "There is no other."

American readers of all interests found satisfaction in the books of the era. Spy novels, thrilling chronicles of the Cold War and espionage, became a new genre for a new age. James Bond, Ian Fleming's master spy, liked his martinis "shaken, not stirred," his women elegant, and his Russian opponents on ice. Bond's motto may

MISHA DEFECTS

At age 26, Mikhail Baryshnikov was the star of the Soviet Union's Kirov Ballet. He was unhappy, however, because the government limited his creative freedom to dance as he pleased. As much as he loved his homeland, Baryshnikov made a decision in favor of his art. On June 24, 1974, he defected while he was in Canada performing with the Bolshoi Ballet.

After he defected, Baryshnikov (called "Misha" by his friends and fans) came to the United States and joined the American Ballet Theatre. He later danced with the New York City Ballet and his own Baryshnikov & Co. In 1981, he became the director of the American Ballet Theatre. Misha's dancing and acting have made the ballet more popular with the American public.

CARTOONIST WINS PULITZER PRIZE

Garry Trudeau, the creator of the satirical cartoon *Doonesbury*, was the first comic-strip artist to win the Pulitzer Prize for editorial cartooning (1975). The strip pokes fun at public figures and politicians. It has been moved to the editorial pages of many newspapers whose readers think the material too biting for the comics pages.

Trudeau suspended the strip from January 1, 1983, to September 30, 1984. Upon its return, it was published in about 775 newspapers. In 1983, Trudeau and composer Elizabeth Swados based a Broadway musical on the strip.

well have been the title of one of Fleming's most popular books, *You Only Live Twice. The Spy Who Came in from the Cold* and other novels by John Le Carré put the Cold War in a grim, less fantastic light.

Many leading writers of this period dealt with themes of alienation and isolation in their fiction. John Updike, for example, continued his life saga of a prototypical modern American male, the anxiety-ridden Rabbit Angstrom, in his 1971 book *Rabbit Redux.* Saul Bellow won a Pulitzer Prize for "the human understanding and subtle analysis of contemporary culture" in his 1964 novel *Herzog.* The main character is a man struggling to face an unjust world. Philip Roth in *Portnoy's Complaint* and Bernard Malamud in *The Fixer* also featured characters who are searching for a meaning in life. Thomas Pynchon in *Gravity's Rainbow* and Kurt Vonnegut Jr. in *Slaughterhouse-Five* explored the problems created by life in a modern, technological society.

Historical fiction underwent change during the 1960s and early 1970s. John Fowles's powerful and richly textured *The French Lieutenant's Woman* confronted "19th century sensualism with 20th century existential freedom," according to *Life* magazine; "The age of Victoria meets the age of Aquarius." Isaac Bashevis Singer, whose writing was translated from Yiddish, wrote historical novels chronicling the life of European Jews during the nineteenth and twentieth centuries. At the same time, Singer treated the social issues of discrimination. E. L. Doctorow's *Ragtime* took a realistic look at racial prejudice in America in the early twentieth century. William Styron explored the slavery issue in *The Confessions of Nat Turner,* a fictional account of an actual slave revolt in 1831. James Clavell in *Tai-Pan* and James Michener in *Centennial* offered epic-length novels that gave historical fiction new depth as a serious literary form.

Less serious works continued to top the best-seller lists. Harold Robbins and Jacqueline Susann pulled one steamy million-seller after another out of their typewriters. Millions of Americans wept over Erich Segal's tale of love thwarted by death in *Love Story.* And thriller fans found deranged demons and unkind sharks aplenty in William Peter Blatty's *The Exorcist* and Peter Benchley's *Jaws.*

Issues of the Day

Writers of both fiction and nonfiction cast a critical and often disillusioned eye on the events of the period. The Kennedy assassination unleashed a flood of books on the young president and his untimely death, including Arthur Schlesinger's sober *A Thousand Days,* Mark Lane's conspiracy discussion *Rush to Judgment,* and William Manchester's definitive *The Death of a President.* Joe McGinnis shocked the nation with *The Selling of the President,* an exposé of how America's perception of Nixon had been cynically manipulated during the 1968 presidential campaign. Norman Mailer, in his fictional *Why Are We in Vietnam?* added to the angry chorus of voices opposing the Vietnam War.

The experiences of blacks were treated by, among others, Malcolm

X in his autobiography and by Maya Angelou in her autobiographical *I Know Why the Caged Bird Sings*. In her work, Angelou described her childhood in segregated Arkansas. James Baldwin also explored black issues in his autobiographical essay *No Name in the Street*.

During the sixties, frank books on sexuality and sexual behavior helped encourage a new openness. For example, *Human Sexual Response* by researchers William Masters and Virginia Johnson gave new hope to people who suffered from sexual dysfunctions.

Publishers responded to the women's movement by inventing a new category of books: women's literature. The exhaustive *Our Bodies, Ourselves* offered women a new perspective on social and medical issues. Kate Millett explored *Sexual Politics*. Susan Brownmiller's *Against Our Will: Men, Women, and Rape* argued that "sexual force is a pervasive process of intimidation that affects all women," whether or not accompanied by violence. *The Female Eunuch*, by Germaine Greer, was part of the second "feminist wave."

Television

THE INFLUENCE OF TELEVISION

"Television's remarkable performance in communicating news of President Kennedy's assassination and the events that followed was a source of sober satisfaction to all Americans," declared President Johnson. ". . . Television provided a personal experience which all could share, . . . a unifying bond which all could feel."

Tied by electronic bonds, Americans together mourned the death and watched the burial of the president. Television's power lay in its

Decline and Fall?

Once everyone in America has a television, will newspapers and magazines be doomed to extinction, like dinosaurs and the Pony Express? Will computer printers and cathode ray displays speed the demise of the printed word?

These nagging questions became critical in the late sixties, especially after the revered weekly magazine *Saturday Evening Post* folded after 148 years of publication. "Television threatens to engulf the written word like a blob from outer space," wrote Stewart Alsop in *Newsweek*. "The decay of the written word, of which the *Saturday Evening Post*'s death is a symbol, is surely a tragedy, and maybe not a very small tragedy either."

A sad statistic proved Alsop's point: more than 320 magazines and daily newspapers folded during the decade. Some undoubtedly deserved their fate; others had boasted a worthy history. The 77-year-old Indianapolis *Times* had once won a Pulitzer Prize for an exposé of the Ku Klux Klan. By the time its presses stopped their final run, New York's *World Journal Tribune* represented a blend of 13 former dailies. One of them had sent British

▼ ▼ ▼

More than 320 magazines and daily newspapers folded during the decade.

explorer Sir Henry Morton Stanley to Africa in search of David Livingstone; American literary figures Mark Twain and Henry James and sportswriter Red Smith had contributed to others. All were now history, and the nation was poorer for their passing. Could television take their place?

ability to show dramatic events as they happened. Viewers watched the funerals of Dr. Martin Luther King Jr. and Robert Kennedy, and they wept. Almost as one, Americans were repulsed by television pictures showing the horror of war in Vietnam, the devastation caused by urban violence, and the brutality of police beating demonstrators outside the 1968 Democratic convention in Chicago. In the same way, they were together entranced by the otherworldly images of *Apollo 11*'s landing on the moon.

There was another side to television's role as a unifying bond, of course: its power to mold public opinion. Some Americans—even President Johnson, when it suited him—argued that television networks misused their influence.

President Nixon and his outspoken vice president Spiro Agnew denounced the "liberal bias" of news about the Vietnam War. Agnew took the offensive, calling television executives "curled-lip boys in eastern ivory towers" and their news reports "misleading."

Agnew's colorful barbs, however, served only to highlight television's new role in American society. By 1969, 95 percent of American homes had televisions, and 40 percent of those were color sets. Never before in history could so many people stand before "the window of the world."

During this time, the airwaves were dominated by the three major networks: ABC, CBS, and NBC. The potential for diversity represented by cable television remained years away. Meanwhile, the turbulence and images of the times emerged with near hypnotic power in living rooms across the nation.

Escapism Versus Realism

Television captured the full range of human experience. After enduring grim news reports about the Vietnam War, viewers could escape to the world of situation comedies, musical variety programs, and dramas. But even entertainment programming began to be affected by the social and political concerns of the time.

Some programs—the family comedy *My Three Sons*, for example, or the musical program *The Lawrence Welk Show*—emphasized traditional American values. Shows such as these seemed to deny that any social changes were taking place at all. Others, such as *M*A*S*H*, a situation comedy set

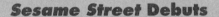

Sesame Street Debuts

A new concept in television programming for children appeared in 1969. *Sesame Street* was developed by the Children's Television Workshop for public television (PBS). The goal of the show was to educate preschool children while entertaining them.

A typical *Sesame Street* program is an hour long. It is fast-paced for the short attention span of preschoolers, with many brief segments of cartoons, short films, and vignettes. Jim Henson's Muppets and recurring child and adult characters are featured in the "neighborhood" setting. Besides working on reading and simple math skills, the show aims to teach relationships, shapes, good social skills, and cultural diversity.

Sesame Street is viewed by millions of children in the United States and in nearly 60 other countries. It has won many awards for outstanding educational programming.

during the Korean War, used humor to attack or make fun of old-fashioned ways of thinking. Still other shows began to emphasize the key role of minorities in America. The situation comedy *Chico and the Man,* the spy drama *Mission: Impossible,* and the science-fiction drama *Star Trek* featured prominent cast members who were Hispanic, black, and Asian.

Though constantly torn between the desire to be entertaining and the need to be relevant, the best shows of the period achieved both. Yet a glimpse at viewers' favorites illustrates how the interests of the networks and their audiences evolved during the turbulent sixties and early seventies. From 1964 to 1966, the old-fashioned western *Bonanza* was the top-rated

Late-Night TV King Johnny Carson

◄ Hubert Humphrey (right), vice president under Lyndon Johnson from 1965 to 1969, visited host Johnny Carson during a *Tonight Show* program in the fall of 1966.

NBC's *The Tonight Show* was a staple in the diet of late-night television viewers long before Johnny Carson took over as its host in 1962. But Carson's sly humor and perfect timing soon made him "television's undisputed Captain Midnight," in the words of one journalist. Mixing sophisticated wit with boyish charm, Carson regularly drew more than a third of all nightly television viewers—10 million by 1968. He was well paid for his efforts. After a much-publicized and closely followed salary dispute in 1967, Carson's annual earnings topped $1 million. In return, he made *The Tonight Show* NBC's largest money-maker.

With Carson as the host for 30 years, *The Tonight Show* became an American institution. Teamed with long-time sidekick Ed McMahon and band-leader Doc Severinsen, Carson developed a trademark formula that skillfully combined the familiar with the unexpected. His comic timing was displayed nightly in opening monologues. He was famous for wringing more laughter from a failed joke than from a successful one. Carson was also known for showcasing the talents of young comedians. Joan Rivers, David Letterman, Jay Leno, and Roseanne Arnold are just a few of many comics who credit him with much of their success.

Whatever the sources of Carson's appeal, millions of fans habitually ended their day watching Johnny talk to vice presidents, famous movie stars, and nameless people with off-beat talents. Carson's reign ended in 1992 when he decided to retire as host of *The Tonight Show.*

show, followed in 1967 by the down-home humor of *The Andy Griffith Show,* with its shady small-town streets, good-hearted sheriff, and friendly neighborhood filling station.

In 1968 and 1969, however, top billing went to the wacky *Laugh-In,* presided over by comedians Dan Rowan and Dick Martin. A fast-paced and impeccably timed variety show, *Laugh-In* featured hilarious slapstick comedy and biting satire. The next year, *Marcus Welby, M.D.*—featuring a grandfatherly figure who solved all problems, medical and otherwise—won the ratings race. The last five years of the period—from 1971 to 1975—were owned by *All in the Family,* an abrasive, controversial comedy about a right-wing bigot and his working-class family, which included his long-haired liberal son-in-law.

Film

MOVIES: FROM INNOCENCE TO EXPERIENCE

In 1964 the Academy Award for best picture was won by *My Fair Lady,* a traditional big-budget musical with a heart-warming ending. Adapted from a George Bernard Shaw play about a British gentleman who turns a Cockney flower girl into an upper-class lady, the movie featured lively, romantic songs such as "I Could Have Danced All Night" and "I've Grown Accustomed to Her Face." In stark contrast, the winner of the best picture award in 1975 cried out

against social injustice. In *One Flew over the Cuckoo's Nest,* the heroes are the inmates of an insane asylum who attempt to establish their own individuality in an oppressive and dehumanizing environment. From this admittedly slim evidence alone, one can safely conclude that something dramatic happened to America in the interim.

It did, of course, and the movies of the era tell the tale. The wonder of modern technology dominated Stanley Kubrick's visionary *2001: A Space Odyssey.* This science-fiction movie is considered by many to be one of the most masterful yet complex films ever made. Tracing human history from ancient times through a trip to the planet Jupiter, the film overwhelmed viewers with its startling images, dominating sound track, and impressive special effects.

Technology appeared even more powerful in Kubrick's *Dr. Strangelove, or How I Learned to Stop Worrying and Love the Bomb.* Too powerful, in fact: this black comedy about the destruction of the earth ends with the world being blown apart by a nuclear bomb. The world barely survives in *A Clockwork Orange.* Also directed by Kubrick, this 1971 film repelled viewers with its graphic vision of a future society where gangs of juvenile thugs roam freely, ravaging citizens at will.

A less gruesome variety of crime was featured in the bloody but romantic and hugely popular *Bonnie and Clyde,* a 1967 film starring Warren Beatty and Faye Dunaway. It became the most successful crime film of the sixties. In the 1970s, director Francis Ford Coppola told the story of a Mafia family in *The Godfather* (1972) and *The Godfather, Part II* (1974). His gripping story of the criminal world received rave reviews for its artistry.

Screams and gunfire were not the only sounds to emerge from Hollywood. *A Man for All Seasons*, the 1966 film about the English philosopher and churchman Sir Thomas More, was "one of the most elegant and intellectual serious films ever produced by an American studio," in the opinion of one reviewer. Most critics agreed, however, that Sweden's Ingmar Bergman was the serious film genius of the era, producing intellectual favorites such as *Smiles of a Summer Night* and *Winter Light*.

Issues of Race and Youth

One of the most pressing social issues of the sixties, the explosive racial tension between blacks and whites, received serious attention in the powerful 1967 film *In the Heat of the Night*, which starred Sidney Poitier and Rod Steiger. Another pervasive social phenomenon, the counterculture, also appeared on the silver screen. *Easy Rider* was the first major movie about the counterculture, and it became one of the most influential films of the era. It followed the trail of two long-haired, drug-dealing, motorcycle-riding hippies as they endured constant harassment by unsympathetic "square" adults. *The Graduate* pushed America's sexual boundaries with its depiction of the older generation trying to deny true love and happiness to the young.

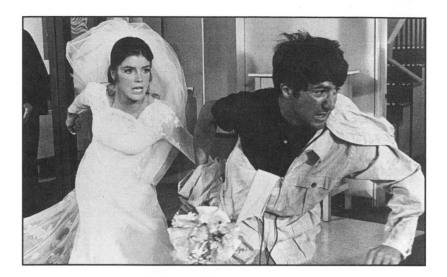

Theater

THE THEATER CONTINUES TO ENTERTAIN

The rise of television, many feared, would doom Broadway theater to eternal darkness. That did not happen. To be sure, the number of musicals on Broadway declined from 36 in 1961 to 28 in 1969. Yet two of the most popular musicals of all time ran during this period: *Fiddler on the Roof* premiered in 1964, and *A Chorus Line* opened in 1975.

The brilliant careers of Stephen Sondheim and Jerome Robbins were two reasons why musicals thrived during the 1960s and early 1970s. Sondheim first wrote song lyrics to go with Leonard Bernstein's music in the 1957 smash hit *West Side Story*. Then Sondheim wrote both lyrics and music for several popular and innovative musicals, including *Company* and *A Little Night Music*. Robbins, most critics agree, is the most distinguished choreographer of ballet and musical theater America has ever produced. He too collaborated

▲ In this scene from the movie *The Graduate*, Dustin Hoffman (right), who is too late to stop the woman he loves (Katharine Ross) from marrying the man her parents want her to marry, escapes from the church with her *after* the ceremony.

ACADEMY AWARD WINNERS FOR BEST PICTURE, 1964–1975

1964	*My Fair Lady*
1965	*The Sound of Music*
1966	*A Man for All Seasons*
1967	*In the Heat of the Night*
1968	*Oliver!*
1969	*Midnight Cowboy*
1970	*Patton*
1971	*The French Connection*
1972	*The Godfather*
1973	*The Sting*
1974	*The Godfather, Part II*
1975	*One Flew over the Cuckoo's Nest*

▼ The Broadway musical *Hair*, which portrayed hippies of the 1960s, was one of the first theatrical plays to adapt rock music for the stage.

on *West Side Story*, creating a new form of musical by integrating dance with the story line. Robbins both choreographed and directed *Fiddler on the Roof*. He staged *Funny Girl* in the same year.

Man of La Mancha, a musical version of the Don Quixote story, illustrates another reason musicals flourished. The production stirred America's deep optimism. Its popular song "The Impossible Dream" encouraged millions to pursue their highest goals whatever the cost.

Problems of the modern day were tackled in the musical *Hair*, which came to Broadway in 1968. With songs such as "Aquarius" and "Good Morning, Starshine," the play examined the encounter between hippies and a young man who has been drafted for Vietnam.

One of the most important playwrights of the sixties was Edward Albee, whose plays explored the often painful absurdity of modern

life. The feuding couples in *Who's Afraid of Virginia Woolf?* exposed the grim side of middle-class life. Two of Albee's plays, *A Delicate Balance* and *Seascape*, won Pulitzer prizes. Tom Stoppard won a Tony Award for his 1966 play *Rosencrantz and Guildenstern Are Dead*, an innovative retelling of William Shakespeare's play *Hamlet* through the eyes of Hamlet's court attendants.

The prolific Harold Pinter wrote plays full of sinister threats, long silences, and suspenseful plots. His most significant works of the period include his subtle and controversial *The Homecoming; Old Times*, a poignant display of memory's power to wound; and *No Man's Land*, a play about the curious relationship between two men, one who failed in life and one who succeeded.

For his part, Neil Simon made certain Broadway audiences had something to laugh about. His 1965 play *The Odd Couple* became a film and a long-running television series. Simon's *Plaza Suite* and *The Sunshine Boys* were plays that eventually were made into movies. He also wrote the book for the successful musical *Promises, Promises*, which opened on Broadway in 1968.

Art

A NEW LOOK IN ART

Between 1964 and 1975, American artists explored innovative forms of expression. Their efforts were in part supported by the National Endowment for the Arts, established in 1965. The relative prosperity of the affluent classes in America also stimulated new interest in viewing and buying art.

One of the most interesting artistic developments of the era involved the blending of art and technology. In the mid-1960s, Robert Rauschenberg helped form an organization called Experiments in Art and Technology (EAT). For two years, more than 30 artists and engineers worked to develop an EAT exhibit for the 1970 World's Fair at Osaka, Japan. The result was a huge success, both technically and artistically. The EAT pavilion encouraged visitors to become actively involved in its space-age atmosphere. A sophisticated light and sound system responded to the movements and sounds created by the spectators. The world's largest spherical mirror created three-dimensional reflections of the audience on the domed ceiling, and a cloud of artificially produced fog hovered over the dome.

Pop Art and Other Trends

Rauschenberg himself was a leader in what was called "popular," or "pop," art. Taking as its subject matter the popular culture of the era, pop art often depicted everyday items such as photographs, brand-name consumer products, and comic strips. One of its purposes was to poke fun at society's obsession with material things.

Rauschenberg used cardboard boxes and newspaper clippings to create elaborate collages. Andy Warhol, the most famous of the pop artists, made realistic silk screens from photographs of items

◀ Pop artist Andy Warhol drew on his background as a commercial artist to create his reproductions of everyday objects and likenesses of famous people.

such as Campbell soup cans. He also made dramatic images of Elizabeth Taylor, Marilyn Monroe, and other famous people. Claes Oldenburg caused viewers to look at familiar objects in new ways. For example, he created soft sculptures of mammoth hamburgers and giant telephones and large-scale reproductions of a three-way electric plug and a toilet bowl.

Minimalism and op, or optical, art were also trends during this time. **Minimalists** and op artists used simple linear and geometric shapes to create their work. For example, minimalist sculptor Donald Judd produced objects such as boxes of steel and aluminum. The paintings of op artist Richard Anuszkiewicz were often alternating patterns that gave the illusion of movement.

In 1972 exhibitions across the country focused on ethnic art: Soviet arts and crafts, Mexican decorative arts, American Indian art, and Eskimo art. The following year, the United States hosted major art shows from the Soviet Union, China, India, and Japan, as Nixon's new policy of **détente** reached the art world.

*"[P*op art is] the use of commercial art as a subject matter in painting. . . . It was hard to get a painting that was despicable enough so that no one would hang it. . . . The one thing everyone hated was commercial art; apparently they didn't hate that enough either.*"*
—Roy Lichtenstein, 1964

SPORTS AND LEISURE

In the old days, professional athletes concentrated on hitting sliders low and away, evading the full-tilt charge of middle linebackers, and keeping their tee shots in the center of the fairway—and they did it for relatively little money.

In the 1960s and 1970s, however, profitable television contracts made sports big-time business and big-time entertainment.

Television fans by the millions tuned in to see whether their favorite teams and athletes would win or lose. Football fans, for example, were thrilled by the outstanding winning effort of powerhouse teams like Vince Lombardi's Green Bay Packers. Fight fans were drawn to watch the hard-

AT A GLANCE

▶ **The Business of Sports**

▶ **Boxing Champions**

▶ **Baseball Dynasties and Superstars**

▶ **College and Pro Football**

▶ **Top Court Champions**

▶ **Top Star for Top Basketball Team**

hitting performances of heavyweight champion Muhammad Ali on closed-circuit television and by satellite.

During this time, both professional team owners and individual players profited from the large sums paid by television networks for every sport from golf and tennis to baseball and basketball. Superstars and team dynasties emerged, to the delight of sports fans throughout the country.

Even though more Americans than ever watched sports during the sixties and early seventies, they also discovered the virtues of keeping fit. By the mid-1970s, the obsession with fitness reached its peak as a jogging craze swept the nation.

DATAFILE

Sports

World records as of 1975	Men	Women
Track and field		
100-yd. dash	9.0″	10.0″
Mile	3′49.4″	4′28.5″
High jump	7.5 ft.	6.4 ft.
Swimming		
100-m. freestyle	51.11″	56.22″

Leisure

	1965	1975
Average workweek	41.2 hrs.	39.5 hrs.
Attendance		
Baseball (major leagues)	20.3 mil.	30.4 mil.
Football (NFL)	4.6 mil.	10.2 mil.
National parks	36.6 mil.	58.8 mil.
Bicycle sales	6.9 mil.	7.3 mil.

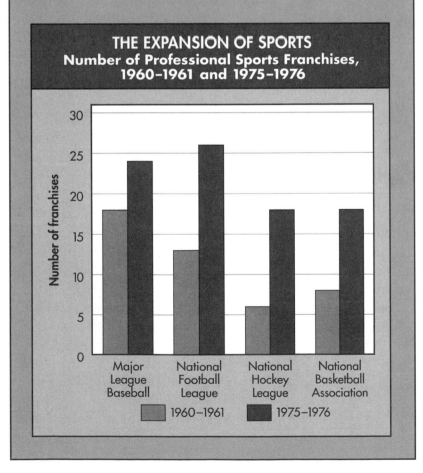

THE EXPANSION OF SPORTS
Number of Professional Sports Franchises, 1960–1961 and 1975–1976

(Bar graph showing Number of franchises for: Major League Baseball, National Football League, National Hockey League, National Basketball Association; comparing 1960–1961 and 1975–1976.)

THE BUSINESS OF SPORTS

Between 1964 and 1975 there was an unprecedented increase in the number of professional sports teams. By the mid-1970s, almost every sizable city in the nation had at least one big-league sports team. Most major cities had two or three, and some—New York and Chicago, for example—had half a dozen. After a second rival professional basketball league was formed in 1967, the sport had a total of 25 teams. In 1976 the leagues merged into one 22-team league. The National Football League (NFL) expanded to 16 teams in 1967, then added 10 teams by merging with the young American Football League (AFL) in 1970.

Why? **Entrepreneurs** recognized that professional sports was a highly profitable business. Baseball attendance, for example, climbed from 224 million during the 1960s to 330 million in the 1970s. But most of the money came from television revenues. Pete Rozelle, the pro football commissioner, made sports history in the early seventies by signing multimillion-dollar television contracts that earned stupendous sums for team owners by 1974. The owner of the Dallas Cowboys described Rozelle as "the greatest salesman in the history of the world."

Before owners had a chance to gloat, however, players began to seek their fair share. The New York Jets, for example, stunned the sports world in 1964 by signing the University of Alabama's standout quarterback Joe Namath for

FIRST WOMAN IN THE KENTUCKY DERBY

The first woman ever to ride in a Kentucky Derby was Diane Crump on May 2, 1970. Riding the thoroughbred Fathom, Crump finished fifteenth out of 17 jockeys.

the unheard-of sum of $427,000. By the mid-seventies, at least 150 baseball, football, basketball, and hockey players were earning more than $100,000 per year. Top stars earned substantially more: basketball's Wilt Chamberlain ($600,000), baseball's Dick Allen ($233,000), hockey's Bobby Hull ($300,000), and football's O. J. Simpson ($250,000).

Many players received far more than just a salary. Lew Alcindor (who changed his name to Kareem Abdul-Jabbar in 1971) was offered 3,500 head of cattle on his own 40,000-acre ranch, in addition to a million-dollar signing bonus and salary, to play basketball. As TV exposure made athletes into media stars, top players boosted their incomes by endorsing products, starring in movies, and moonlighting as sports commentators.

The king of athletic entrepreneurs, without a doubt, was Arnold Palmer, the leading money winner in professional golf during the early 1960s. Palmer used his winnings to build a business empire. In 1966 companies owned or licensed by Palmer reported sales of almost $15 million.

Over time, however, the struggle between owners and players for control of the economic pie began to change the business of professional sports. This change was very evident in baseball. Traditionally, all baseball contracts included a reserve clause that allowed owners to do what they wanted with a player—keep him, trade him, sell him, or let him go. In 1969 the player Curt Flood began a legal fight to allow baseball players to become **free agents** after their

contracts expired. He did not want to be traded unless he agreed.

Although it was not until the late 1970s that players won the right to be free agents under certain conditions, their voices were starting to be heard. In 1972 the first baseball players' strike canceled the first 13 games of the season. During this time, the Players Association started working hard for players' rights. The group gained the right to have an outside party decide disputes between players and owners. The owners' grip on players was no longer quite so tight.

HEAVYWEIGHT BOXING CHAMPIONS

By the time Cassius Clay fought Sonny Liston for the heavyweight championship of the world in 1964, Clay had already compiled an impressive record: 108 amateur victories, four national championships, an Olympic gold medal, and 19 straight professional victories. Clay was a superb athlete and an elegant boxer. He moved with the grace of a ballet dancer and punched so fast that the eye could not follow. But he also became a social symbol. Two days after his astounding defeat of the powerful Liston in only six rounds, Clay announced his conversion to the Black Muslim faith, taking the name Muhammad Ali.

After nine successful title defenses in the next three years, Ali defiantly refused to be drafted into the Army. He gave as his reason his commitment to peace as a Black Muslim minister. As a result, Ali was stripped of his boxing license and title by the sport's governing commissions. He was also convicted of draft dodging. He appealed his conviction, which was overturned by the U.S. Supreme Court in 1971. The previous year, a federal court ruled that Ali's license should be reinstated.

Meanwhile, "Smokin' Joe" Frazier, another Olympic champion, emerged with the title. It was Frazier who thwarted Ali's 1971 comeback effort in a memorable fight at Madison Square Garden. This bout was seen by more than 300 million people through closed-circuit television shown in movie theaters. In 1973, however, Frazier fell to the enormous punching power of George Foreman, yet another Olympic boxing champion. Ali regained his title in a stunning triumph over Foreman in Zaire in 1974.

Muhammad Ali: "I Am the Greatest"

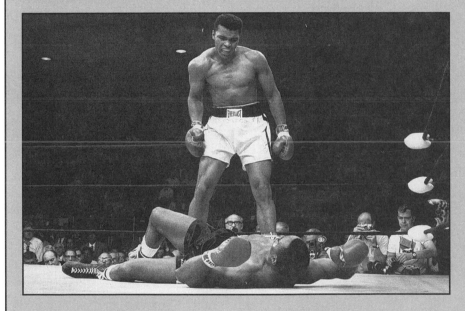

▲ In their second meeting, in May 1965, Ali knocked out Liston in the first round.

"He came into the world with a good body and a big head," remarked Cassius Clay Sr. of his son the boxer. The elder Clay was correct on both counts. Muhammad Ali's physical prowess was beyond question, as dozens of baffled opponents found out. He moved around the ring with exceptional speed, dodging and punching, fists darting like the tongue of a cobra. In his prime, Ali completely dominated boxing. He was a study in poise and complete, utter confidence.

Ali's worldwide fame, however, came as much from his "big head" as from his good body. Perhaps the world's first heavyweight poet, Ali peppered the air with boasts and bombast. "Float like a butterfly—sting like a bee," was his theme verse, to which he added in later years, "That's why they call me Muhammad Ali." Then came the often-repeated claim "I am the king— I am the greatest," daring anyone to prove him wrong. At first, sportswriters called him "Cassius the Brashest," but soon his feats in the ring turned jeers to cheers.

Ali became an inspiration outside the boxing ring, too. After he was convicted of avoiding the military draft because of his beliefs as a Black Muslim, he gained a large following among those working for social change. He became a symbol of pride for blacks and for those working in the anti–Vietnam War movement.

Baseball

BASEBALL DYNASTIES AND SUPERSTARS

Between 1936 and 1953, the New York Yankees won the World Series an unbelievable 13 times, including a never-equaled 5 World Series titles in a row. Most baseball experts believe free agency and other changes in the game will prevent future teams from ever again achieving that level of domination.

During the late sixties and early seventies, two teams—the Baltimore Orioles and the Oakland Athletics—established impressive dynasties, though, as they earned their own prominent places in the record books of America's national pastime.

Between 1966 and 1974, the Baltimore Orioles won two division championships, five American League pennants, and two World Series titles. Their pitching staff was one of the best ever assembled, led by ace Jim Palmer, who anchored a starting rotation that had four 20-game winners in 1971. Frank Robinson, Baltimore's outstanding right fielder, pounded 49 homers in 1966. That year he won the triple crown, leading the league in batting average, runs batted in, and home runs. The Oriole defense featured the incomparable Brooks Robinson at third base. Robinson earned the American League Gold Glove Award for third basemen every year from 1960 to 1975, and he won the 1971 World Series almost single-handedly with his brilliant defensive play.

The Oakland Athletics clinched their third straight year as baseball's world champions with a four-games-to-one World Series victory over the Los Angeles Dodgers in 1974. The mustache-laden A's had their share of superstar starting pitchers, including crafty Catfish Hunter and the fast Vida Blue. But they also had very talented relief pitchers, including Rollie Fingers, whose mustache wound upward into giant handlebars. The A's dominant hitter was slugger Reggie Jackson. Many people believe that the A's would have won four World Series in a row had Jackson not been injured early in the 1971 playoffs.

Individual Triumphs

As the Orioles and the A's built their dynasties, individual players also stood out as superstars. The

Little League Opens to Girls

When the organization was founded in 1939, Little League was limited to boys ages 9 to 12. In June 1974, however, the group yielded to pressure from advocates of women's rights. Little League opened its enrollment to girls—because of "the changing social climate."

In December 1974, President Gerald Ford made the policy federal law when he signed legislation permitting girls to compete in Little League.

◀ On April 30, 1961, Willie Mays, of the San Francisco Giants, hit his fourth home run of the day in a game with the Milwaukee Braves. It was just one of many baseball milestones in Mays's Hall of Fame career, which lasted into the 1970s.

story of pitcher Sandy Koufax is a chronicle of triumph and disappointment. Koufax, who pitched for the Dodgers from 1955 to 1966, was a brilliant left-hander. His overpowering fastballs fanned 2,396 batters in 2,325 innings, a remarkable accomplishment of more than one strikeout per inning. He won three Cy Young awards and pitched four no-hitters, including a perfect game on September 9, 1965, against the Chicago Cubs. Midway through his career, however, Koufax was forced to retire as a result of an arthritic elbow.

Sporting News named Willie Mays baseball's Player of the Decade for the 1960s, but that merely confirmed what baseball fans already knew. The Say Hey Kid, always a crowd favorite, was one of the top baseball players of the twentieth century. In a career spanning almost two decades, Mays belted a career total of 660 home runs, recorded 3,283 hits, and won 12 straight Gold Glove awards for outfielders.

Roberto Clemente, the Pittsburgh Pirates' splendid right fielder from 1955 until 1972, is another member of the exclusive 3,000-hit club—but barely. A complete ball player, Clemente could throw strikes to home plate from 460 feet away. His 3,000th hit came in the fourth inning of the final game of the 1972 season. It was the last hit of his career. Tragically, he was killed shortly after the season ended in a plane crash while flying with supplies to aid earthquake victims in Nicaragua. The following year, baseball officials waived the five-year waiting period and elected him into the Hall of Fame.

Two individual achievements during the summer of 1974 also rewrote baseball's record books. Hank Aaron hit his 715th home run, besting the great Babe Ruth's 39-year-old record of 714 career

JERRIE MOCK FLIES SOLO AROUND THE WORLD

On April 17, 1964, Jerrie Mock became the first woman to fly an airplane around the world solo. The 38-year-old homemaker flew the more than 23,000 miles in 29 days, stopping 21 times along the way.

▶ When Atlanta Braves' outfielder Hank Aaron hit his 715th career home run in a game with the Los Angeles Dodgers, he broke Babe Ruth's record of 714, which had been on the books since 1935.

homers. By the time his 20-year career ended in 1976, Aaron recorded 3,771 hits—third highest in history—and belted 755 home runs. This last achievement is not likely to be topped anytime soon.

Also in 1974, the fleet-footed Lou Brock of the St. Louis Cardinals stole a season-record 118 bases. That record and his career total of 938 stolen bases broke records that had stood for almost half a century. Both of Brock's records have since been broken by Rickey Henderson of the Oakland Athletics.

Golf

THE CHANGING OF THE GUARD IN GOLF

Between 1964 and 1975, the world's fairways and putting greens were dominated by one man: Jack Nicklaus. He was the leading money winner in 1964 and in 1975 and for five years in between. During his first ten years as a professional golfer, he won $1.5 million.

Nicklaus not only had great power to drive the ball down the fairway but also had the ability to block out all distractions and putt well on the greens. Few courses were able to tame the Golden Bear, who by 1975 was almost unanimously judged the greatest golfer who had ever lived. He had already won 16 major tournaments, including an unprecedented 5 Masters championships. Only Nicklaus had ever won all four of golf's major tournaments—the U.S. Open, the British Open, the Masters, and the PGA (Professional Golfers Association) Championship—at least twice.

Although Arnold Palmer won most of his major championships in the late 1950s and early 1960s, he continued through the 1960s and early 1970s to thrill his fans with his go-for-broke style of golf. Palmer was a superb golfer: his wins in four Masters, two British Opens, and one U.S. Open attest to that fact. He was also one of the most popular players ever to compete in golf or any other game. His odds-defying brand of playing became legendary, as did his uncanny ability to turn certain defeat into impossible victory. When television began broadcasting golf in the 1960s, Palmer became an instant hero whose legions of fans were quickly dubbed "Arnie's Army." Both Palmer and Nicklaus used their winnings from golf to establish numerous thriving business enterprises.

COLLEGE AND PRO FOOTBALL

Between 1964 and 1975, both individual stars and powerhouse teams increased the interest of the fans in college and professional football. Many stars who excelled in their college playing days were lured by high money offers to sign up for the professional teams' player draft. Team owners wanted big-name college stars to turn pro to attract crowds to their stadiums and to gain viewers for the games on television.

The Professional Sport

In 1967 Vince Lombardi's Green Bay Packers clinched their third consecutive NFL championship. The Packers' old-fashioned, hard-hitting style of play had set them firmly atop the gritty world of professional football. In many ways, the solid, hard-working team embodied the best of America in the early 1960s. Around the same time, Cleveland Browns' running back Jim Brown, considered by many to be the greatest back who ever lived, retired. In 1966, his final season, he set almost every rushing record in the books: an average of 133 yards per game, 6.4 yards per carry, and a total of 1,863 yards. Brown's career average of 5.2 yards per carry remains the highest in history, and his career total of 12,312 yards was then a record. His place in football history was challenged in the 1970s by O. J. Simpson, the greatest college player of the sixties, who rushed for 250 yards in one game and a total of 2,003 yards as a Buffalo Bill in 1973.

The workhorse world of Brown and the Packers was rapidly changing, however. The pervasive influence of television made media superstars out of top players such as the New York Jets' flamboyant quarterback "Broadway Joe" Namath. In addition, the intense bidding war between the NFL and the

▼ O. J. Simpson (carrying the ball in the photo at left) and Joe Namath (handing off the ball in the photo at right) were just two of the era's college football stars recruited by pro teams for large sums of money and other perks.

► The cost of a 30-second TV commercial shown during the Super Bowl rose dramatically from 1967—the year of Super Bowl I—to 1975 as the popularity of the championship game increased.

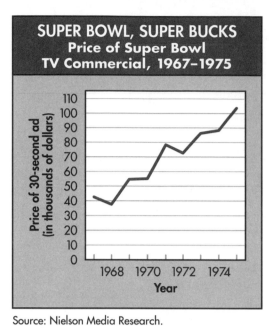

SUPER BOWL, SUPER BUCKS
Price of Super Bowl TV Commercial, 1967–1975

Source: Nielson Media Research.

upstart American Football League sent players' salaries skyrocketing.

To end the competition for players, these two leagues made an agreement in 1966 to merge in 1970. Part of the agreement included the creation of the Super Bowl, which was first played on January 15, 1967, and won by the Green Bay Packers. At first, the Super Bowl was a winner-take-all championship game between the top teams of the NFL and the AFL. Since the merger, it has matched the top teams in the two conferences of the new NFL.

Football became a media sensation. Its appeal was boosted by the brash antics of Namath, who predicted the underdog Jets would defeat the powerful Baltimore Colts in Super Bowl III: "In fact," he said three days before the game, "I guarantee it." The Jets won. By the mid-seventies, the annual Super Bowl was the top-rated television program of the year, attracting more than 50 million viewers in the United States alone. The on-field

success of the Miami Dolphins also helped; they won their second straight Super Bowl in 1974.

The College Game

The legacy of college football during the period was created by three legendary coaches. Woody Hayes, the feisty coach at Ohio State, led his Buckeyes to a perfect 10–0 record during the 1968 season. The Buckeyes also won the Rose Bowl in 1969 and 1972. Hayes's career total of 238 wins put him fourth on the list of all-time football victories in Division I-A of the National Collegiate Athletic Association (NCAA).

The most wins in I-A football history belong to Paul "Bear" Bryant, longtime coach at Alabama, who coached future NFL superstars Joe Namath and Ken Stabler. A rival coach once said that Bryant won "because he coached people, not football." John McKay and the Trojans of the University of Southern California won four Rose Bowl championships during the period, one of which featured the explosive running back O. J. Simpson.

Tennis

TOP COURT CHAMPIONS

Like all other major sports of the era, tennis enjoyed unprecedented growth during the years between 1964 and 1975, as television poured huge sums of money into the game and attracted millions of new fans. Billie Jean King garnered much of the attention during the

early television years, as much for her uninhibited tongue as for her aggressive style of play. She chased the ball and pounded it with ferocious intensity. She was her own worst critic. If she hit the ball badly, she would scream at herself, "Boy, you've got the touch of an ox!"

Though unconventional, and indeed often unwelcome in the once-staid sport of tennis, her style of play won her dozens of matches and millions of fans. After King won the U.S. Open, Wimbledon, and Australian championships in 1967, she was named the world's outstanding female athlete. Her game continued to improve; between 1966 and 1975, she won a total of four U.S. Open championships and six Wimbledon titles.

During this period, Margaret Smith Court, the dominant woman tennis star of the early sixties, also won a number of major championships, including three U.S.

Opens and one Wimbledon. Arthur Ashe, the first black man to be ranked internationally, triumphed over Tom Okker to become the U.S. Open champion in 1968. Australian John Newcombe captured the U.S. Open title twice and Wimbledon three times during the period.

By the mid-1970s, new stars appeared on the horizon. In 1975, after a convincing win at Wimbledon the previous year, Chris Evert took the U.S. Open by storm. It was the first of four consecutive U.S. Open titles for Evert, and she would eventually win five of seven Open titles between 1975 and 1982. In 1974 the 22-year-old men's singles champion at both Wimbledon and the U.S. Open was an argumentative, often arrogant "tennis brat" named Jimmy Connors, the self-styled "bad boy" of tennis. In the years ahead, however, his game continued to heat up while his head cooled off considerably.

BIRTHS . . .

Dwight Gooden, baseball player, 1964
Mario Lemieux, hockey player, 1965
Mike Tyson, boxer, 1966
Steffi Graf, tennis player, 1969

. . . AND DEATHS

Sonja Henie, figure skater, 1969
Rocky Marciano, boxer, 1969
Vince Lombardi, football coach, 1970
Jackie Robinson, baseball player, 1972
Dizzy Dean, baseball player, 1974
Casey Stengel, baseball manager, 1975

TOP STAR FOR TOP BASKETBALL TEAM

When Lew Alcindor joined the varsity basketball team at the University of California at Los Angeles (UCLA), the Bruins squad had already won two straight national championships under legendary coach John Wooden. Even so, the 7-foot 2-inch "Mount Alcindor" created an unprecedented sensation in his first season, 1966–1967. UCLA became "Lew-CLA" and the "University of California at Lew Alcindor." With Alcindor at center, UCLA won 30 games without a loss during 1966–1967, including a third national title. The team extended its win streak to 47 games

before the University of Houston beat UCLA by two points the following year. The excitement over Alcindor, however, did not obscure the fact that Wooden had built a solid, long-term basketball program at UCLA. Between 1964 and 1975, Wooden and the Bruins won 10 of 12 national championships.

When Alcindor—now Kareem Abdul-Jabbar—joined the lowly Milwaukee Bucks of the National Basketball Association (NBA) in 1969, he quickly proved his worth to the team. In 1971, only their third season as an expansion **franchise,** the Bucks won the NBA championship.

The pro basketball team dynasty of the period, however, clearly belonged to Bill Russell and the Boston Celtics. Russell, who had 21,721 rebounds and scored 14,522 points during his career, is considered the finest defensive center in the history of basketball. In 1969, the year Russell retired, he and the Celtics captured the NBA title for the eleventh time in 12 years; the team won the title again in 1974.

Wilt Chamberlain, the most productive offensive player of his day, scored 31,419 points in his career, a total since eclipsed by Abdul-Jabbar. However, Chamberlain still holds almost every other single-game, season, and career scoring and rebounding record. Wilt the Stilt played for three pro teams during his 14-year career and was on two NBA championship teams. A reserved man off the court, Chamberlain transformed the game of basketball with his combination of towering height, overpowering strength, and delicate touch.

Astrodome Built in Houston

The first domed sports arena was the Harris County Domed Stadium—the Houston Astrodome. The $35.5 million arena was built with a permanent roof made of 4,596 plastic skylights and equipped with lights for nighttime sporting events. The Astrodome seats 66,000 spectators and covers 9.5 acres, making it one of the world's largest indoor stadiums.

The first baseball game played in the Astrodome was on April 9, 1965. The Houston Astros beat the New York Yankees 2–1 in a 12-inning exhibition game. Since then, the Astrodome has also been used for football, basketball, boxing, and polo.

WINTER AND SUMMER GAMES

"Who is Billy Mills?" The question raced through the crowd at the 1964 Olympic Games in Tokyo, Japan. Mills, an unknown American distance runner, had just won the 10,000-meter run in one of the most electrifying upsets in Olympic history. For two weeks before the race, not one reporter had asked Mills a single question. Now they crowded around him, besieging him with questions.

"I'm flabbergasted," responded Mills, whose winning time of 28 minutes 24.4 seconds was 46 seconds faster than his previous best. "I can't believe it. I guess I was the only person who thought I had a chance." A Marine Corps officer and 7/16 Sioux Indian, Mills was the first American in history ever to win the Olympic gold medal in the 10,000-meter run.

Pelé: Brazil's National Treasure

◀ In a game with a Mexican team, the Brazilian soccer star Pelé (right) defies a defensive block as he dribbles the ball downfield toward a goal.

Soccer was, and is, the most popular game in the world. Edson Arantes do Nascimento was, and remains, the most popular soccer player of all time. Billions of soccer fans around the world know him simply as Pelé, the Black Pearl of Brazil. The son of a minor-league soccer player, Pelé became an overnight sensation when he led Brazil to a decisive victory over Wales in the 1958 World Cup. The Brazilian government declared Pelé a "national treasure" to prevent him from being traded to a European club for an astronomical sum. He quickly became one of the highest-paid athletes in the world, however, earning a tax-free salary of $500,000 per year. He proved his worth by leading Brazil to victory in the 1962 and 1970 World Cup events.

On the field, his exploits seemed magical. He stalked opponents like a panther. He could spring out of the pack to execute dazzling headers that no one else could reach. He was able to leap high to catch a pass on one thigh, then volley the ball into the goal with the other foot—while still airborne. Pelé's mere presence on a soccer field inspired excellence in his teammates and put his opponents on the defensive.

By the time Pelé retired from World Cup competition in 1971, he had scored 1,086 goals. He continued to play for a Brazilian team until 1974. One year later, he was paid $4.7 million to play for three seasons with the New York Cosmos.

When American Bob Beamon set
the world record for the long jump
on October 18, 1968, many
thought the record would never be
broken. However, nearly 23 years
later, on September 6, 1991,
American Michael Powell
succeeded. He set a new world
record by jumping 29 feet 4 ½
inches—2 inches farther than
Beamon.

Between 1964 and 1975, other Olympic Games produced moments just as dramatic. Women's figure skating at the 1968 winter games in Grenoble, France, was dominated by Peggy Fleming. First, she built up a huge scoring lead after completing the compulsory moves selected by the judges. Then her spectacular free-skating routine ensured her victory. She was the only American gold medal winner at Grenoble. The powerful French skier Jean Claude Killy garnered the grand slam in men's skiing, winning gold medals in the downhill, the slalom, and the giant slalom. After his stunning victory, "the party went on for two and a half days," Killy later recalled.

The 1968 summer games in Mexico City, Mexico, was the site of several memorable events for American athletes. Tommie Smith and John Carlos, both students at San Jose State College and members of the Olympic Project for Human Rights, placed first and third

▶ Gold medalist Tommie
Smith (center) and bronze
medalist John Carlos (right) give
the black-power salute during the
awards ceremony for the 200-
meter dash at the 1968 Olympic
Games in Mexico City, Mexico.

in the 200-meter dash. Smith, an extraordinary runner who already held 11 world records, set yet another in his dash to the gold. As they stood on the victory stand during "The Star-Spangled Banner," Smith and Carlos each raised one gloved fist in a black-power salute. They wanted to show their disdain for the racial policies of the United States. "White America will only give us credit for an Olympic victory," Carlos told reporters. "They'll say I'm an American, but if I did something bad, they'd say I was a Negro." Their eloquent, non-violent protest was poorly received by Olympic and American officials; both were suspended from the games.

Also in Mexico City, Dick Fosbury, the American originator of an unconventional technique for high jumping dubbed the "Fosbury Flop," won the gold medal in that event. Bob Beamon's unbelievable 29-foot 2½-inch long jump won him the gold medal and was hailed by many as the greatest athletic achievement of all time. Beamon's jump added 21¾ inches to the world record; he beat his closest competitor by 2½ feet.

American swimmer Mark Spitz splashed into the pool at the 1972 summer games in Munich, West Germany, and emerged with seven Olympic medals—an Olympic record. Along the way, Spitz also set new world records in each event he entered. The American basketball team, however, was defeated by the USSR in a controversial gold-medal match. The loss ended a 62-game winning streak for the Americans, which they had achieved during eight Olympic Games.

COLORFUL STYLES AND FADS

The vocabulary of fashion, like everything else between 1964 and 1975, was a language of extremes. As part of their wide-ranging rebellion against almost everything, young people kicked off a revolution in the fashion world. Women wore miniskirts, which stopped several inches above the knee, and midi coats, which came down to the ankle. Some wore cut-out designs over body stockings and see-through blouses.

Women rediscovered pants— hot pants, bell-bottoms, and pant suits. Some women preferred the boldly patterned and unrestrained clothes made popular by those in the counterculture. Fashion novelties such as disposable paper dresses and Mickey Mouse wristwatches also made an appearance.

Men grew their hair long and joined the "peacock revolution." Dark suits and white shirts were replaced by colorful hip-hugging flared pants. Turtlenecks and brightly colored shirts became popular for men. At this time, the unisex look also became fashionable. It featured clothing that could be worn by either men or women.

The leisure fads of the era were pervasive. Everyone was either throwing a frisbee, riding a skateboard, or simply owning a pet rock— unless, of course, they had a Barbie or a GI Joe doll, a Ouija board, or a James Bond toy: these took precedence. Body painting, macrobiotic foods, underground newspapers, acupuncture, transcendental meditation, and Tarot cards provided welcome diversions for the young **counterculture** crowd. But by the seventies, many Americans were getting serious about life: they were jogging. Was this progress?

▲ Women in miniskirts (left) and young people taking part in "love-ins" (right) were signs of the times during the sixties and early seventies.

NEW WORDS
discotheque
skateboard
psychedelic
miniskirt
guru
preppie

VOICES OF THE ERA

Black is beautiful.

—Black pride slogan, 1960s

The Commission has found no evidence that either Lee Harvey Oswald or Jack Ruby was part of any conspiracy, domestic or foreign, to assassinate President Kennedy.

—Earl Warren,
*Report of the President's Commission
on the Assassination of President Kennedy,* 1964

"*I*'m the only president you've got."

—Lyndon B. Johnson,
press conference, April 27, 1964

"*B*lack power doesn't mean anti-white, violence, separatism or any other racist things the press says it means. It's saying 'Look, buddy, we're not laying a vote on you unless you lay so many schools, hospitals, playgrounds, and jobs on us.'"

—Stokely Carmichael,
interview with *Life* photographer
Gordon Parks, 1967

Be peaceful, be courteous, obey the law, respect everyone; but if someone puts a hand on you, send him to the cemetery.

—Malcolm X,
Malcolm X Speaks, 1965

"*S*o I ask you tonight to join me and march along the road to the future, the road that leads to the Great Society."

—Lyndon B. Johnson,
speech, May 28, 1964

Hell no.
We won't go.

—Antiwar slogan, 1960s

When I stepped out into the bright sunlight from the darkness of the movie house, I had only two things on my mind: Paul Newman and a ride home. I was wishing I looked like Paul Newman—he looks tough and I don't—but I guess my own looks aren't so bad. I have light-brown, almost-red hair and greenish-gray eyes. I wish they were more gray, because I hate most guys that have green eyes, but I have to be content with what I have. My hair is longer than a lot of boys wear theirs, squared off in back and long at the front and sides, but I am a greaser and most of my neighborhood rarely bothers to get a haircut. Besides, I look better with long hair.

—S. E. Hinton, *The Outsiders,* 1967

Nobody can give you freedom. Nobody can give you equality or justice or anything. If you're a man, you take it.

—Malcolm X,
Malcolm X Speaks, 1965

"*N*o more war, war never again."

—Pope Paul VI,
addressing the United Nations, 1965

Probably the most destructive feature of Black Power is its unconscious and often conscious call for retaliatory violence. . . . The problem with hatred and violence is that they intensify the fears of the white majority and leave them less ashamed of their prejudices toward Negroes. In the guilt and confusion confronting our society, violence only adds to the chaos. It deepens the brutality of the oppressor and increases the bitterness of the oppressed. Violence is the antithesis of creativity and wholeness. It destroys community and makes brotherhood impossible.

—Martin Luther King Jr.,
Where Do We Go from Here? 1967

"*Winning isn't everything, it's the only thing.*"

—Vince Lombardi, 1966

"*They nominate a president and he eats the people. We nominate a president and the people eat him.*"

—Abbie Hoffman,
on the nomination of a pig
as the Youth International party
presidential candidate,
Chicago, August 1968

"*Christianity will go. It will vanish and shrink. I needn't argue about that; I'm right and I will be proved right. . . . [The Beatles are] more popular than Jesus now; I don't know which will go first— rock 'n' roll or Christianity.*"

—John Lennon, March 4, 1966

Suppose they gave a war and nobody came.

—Antiwar slogan, 1960s

A segregated school system produces children who, when they graduate, graduate with crippled minds.

—Malcolm X,
Malcolm X Speaks, 1965

Say good night, Dick.
Good night, Dick.

—Dan Rowan and Dick Martin
in *Laugh In*, 1968–1973

Come mothers and fathers,
Throughout the land
And don't criticize
What you can't understand.
Your sons and your daughters
Are beyond your command
Your old road is
Rapidly agin'
Please get out of the new one
If you can't lend your hand
For the times they are a-changin'!

—Bob Dylan,
"The Times They Are A-Changin'," 1964

VOICES OF THE ERA

'GIANT LEAP FOR MANKIND'

Armstrong Takes 1st Step on Moon

—*Chicago Tribune*, July 21, 1969

***S**ock it to me.*

—Popular saying,
late 1960s

KENT STATE RIOT; 4 KILLED

Troops Fight with Students

—*Chicago Tribune*, May 5, 1970

"*A*ll right, Edith, you go right
ahead and do your thing . . . but just
remember that your thing is eggs
over easy and crisp bacon."

—Carroll O'Connor
in *All in the Family*

METS WIN, 5–3, TAKE THE SERIES, AND A GRATEFUL CITY GOES WILD

Fans Storm Field
Thousands Rip Up Turf
After a Late Rally
Defeats Orioles

—*New York Times*, October 17, 1969

WOMEN MAKE POLICY NOT COFFEE

"*G*od knows many of them are fools, and
most of them will be sellouts, but they're a better
generation than we were."

—Lillian Hellman

If you won't hire her,
don't complain about
supporting her.

—Public service ad, 1969

When the moon is in the seventh house
And Jupiter aligns with Mars
Then peace will guide the planets
And love will steer the stars.
This is the dawning of the Age of Aquarius,
The Age of Aquarius.
Harmony and understanding
Sympathy and trust abounding
No more falsehoods or derisions
Golden living dreams of visions
Mystic crystal revelation
The mind's true liberation.

—"Aquarius," by James Rado,
Jerome Ragni,
and Galt MacDermot, 1966

All we are saying
Is give peace a chance.

—John Lennon and Paul McCartney,
"Give Peace a Chance," 1969

I can't believe I ate
the whole thing!

—Alka Seltzer ad, 1971

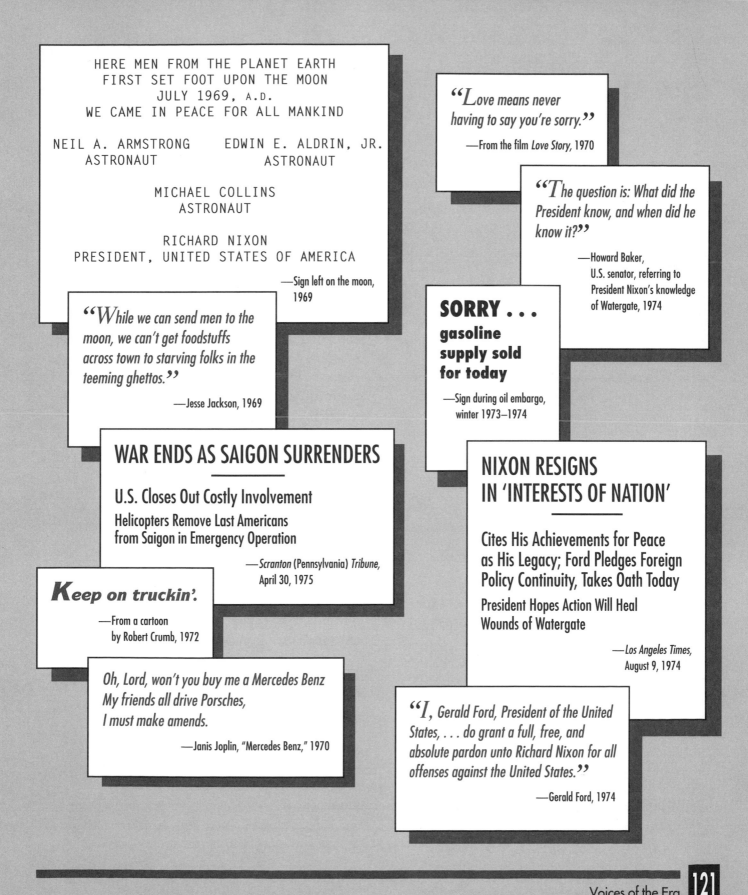

HERE MEN FROM THE PLANET EARTH
FIRST SET FOOT UPON THE MOON
JULY 1969, A.D.
WE CAME IN PEACE FOR ALL MANKIND

NEIL A. ARMSTRONG   EDWIN E. ALDRIN, JR.
ASTRONAUT   ASTRONAUT

MICHAEL COLLINS
ASTRONAUT

RICHARD NIXON
PRESIDENT, UNITED STATES OF AMERICA

—Sign left on the moon,
1969

"While we can send men to the moon, we can't get foodstuffs across town to starving folks in the teeming ghettos."

—Jesse Jackson, 1969

WAR ENDS AS SAIGON SURRENDERS

U.S. Closes Out Costly Involvement

**Helicopters Remove Last Americans
from Saigon in Emergency Operation**

—*Scranton* (Pennsylvania) *Tribune,*
April 30, 1975

Keep on truckin'.

—From a cartoon
by Robert Crumb, 1972

*Oh, Lord, won't you buy me a Mercedes Benz
My friends all drive Porsches,
I must make amends.*

—Janis Joplin, "Mercedes Benz," 1970

"Love means never having to say you're sorry."

—From the film *Love Story,* 1970

"The question is: What did the President know, and when did he know it?"

—Howard Baker,
U.S. senator, referring to
President Nixon's knowledge
of Watergate, 1974

SORRY . . .
gasoline supply sold for today

—Sign during oil embargo,
winter 1973–1974

NIXON RESIGNS IN 'INTERESTS OF NATION'

**Cites His Achievements for Peace
as His Legacy; Ford Pledges Foreign
Policy Continuity, Takes Oath Today**

President Hopes Action Will Heal
Wounds of Watergate

—*Los Angeles Times,*
August 9, 1974

"I, Gerald Ford, President of the United States, . . . do grant a full, free, and absolute pardon unto Richard Nixon for all offenses against the United States."

—Gerald Ford, 1974

Glossary

balance of power: a condition in which nations' political and military might is fairly equal

capital: goods or property accumulated, usually to produce income

capitalism: an economic system controlled by individuals and corporations rather than by government, characterized by open competition in a free market

chlorofluorocarbon: a synthetic chemical used primarily as a coolant, which, when released into the atmosphere, deteriorates the earth's protective ozone layer

counterculture: a culture whose values oppose or conflict with the prevailing, established values of a society

deficit: having more expenses than income

détente: the easing of tension between countries

discrimination: the act of treating people differently for a particular reason, often an unfair one

embargo: an order prohibiting trade, especially the movement of commercial ships

entrepreneur: an individual who organizes, manages, and assumes the risk for a business venture

food chain: an arrangement of a series of organisms in which each eats a smaller one and is, in turn, eaten by a larger one

fossil fuel: a type of fuel, such as gasoline, derived from living matter of a previous geologic era

franchise: the right to own a member team as granted by a league in certain professional sports

free agent: a professional player who is free to sign a contract with any team

genetic engineering: the deliberate alteration of genetic material to prevent hereditary defects

gross national product: the total dollar value of all the goods and services produced in a country in one year

guerrillas: a small, independent band of people who fight as part of a patriotic or revolutionary movement

hallucinatory drugs: mind-altering drugs that affect a person's perceptions of reality

inflation: a general increase in prices and fall in the purchasing value of money in an economy

microprocessor: a semiconductor central processing unit usually contained on a single circuit chip

multinational: operating in two or more countries

nationalism: loyalty and devotion to a nation

nationalize: to transfer ownership of land and property from private owners to the government

poll taxes: taxes formerly levied on every adult as a requirement for voting

privatizing: the process of allowing private ownership, rather than government ownership, of industries and services

recession: a temporary decline in economic activity

referendum: the referring of a proposed public measure to a direct public vote

separatist movement: an organized effort to achieve political, religious, or racial separation

socialism: an economic theory that promotes governmental control of factories and other businesses

software: the programs that enable computers to perform specific tasks

sphere of influence: a territorial area within which the political interests of one nation are dominant

subsidy: a grant or gift of money

Third World: the underdeveloped countries of Asia, Africa, and Latin America

unconstitutional: not in accordance with a particular constitution

utopian community: an ideal living environment where everything is perfect

windfall profits: unexpected profits made by a business

Suggested Readings

General

Abbott, Carl. *Urban America in the Modern Age, 1920 to Present.* H. Davidson, 1987.

Allen, Frederick Lewis. *The Big Change, 1900–1950.* Bantam, 1965.

Blum, Daniel. *A Pictorial History of the Silent Screen.* Grosset & Dunlap, 1953.

Cairns, Trevor. *The Twentieth Century.* Cambridge University Press, 1984.

Cantor, Norman F., and Michael S. Werthman, eds. *The History of Popular Culture.* Macmillan, 1968.

Churchill, Allen. *The Great White Way.* E. P. Dutton, 1962.

Daniels, Roger. *Coming to America: A History of Immigration and Ethnicity in American Life.* HarperCollins, 1990.

Davids, Jules. *America and the World of Our Time.* Random House, 1960.

Ewing, Elizabeth. *History of Twentieth Century Fashion.* Barnes & Noble, 1986.

Filene, Peter G. *Him/Her/Self: Sex Roles in Modern America.* Johns Hopkins University Press, 1986.

Flink, James J. *The Automobile Age.* MIT, 1988.

Freidel, Frank. *America in the Twentieth Century.* Knopf, 1960.

Goff, Richard. *The Twentieth Century: A Brief Global History.* John Wiley, 1983.

Hine, Darlene Clark, ed. *Black Women in American History.* Carlson Publishing, 1990.

Manchester, William. *The Glory and the Dream: A Narrative History of America, 1932–1972.* Little, Brown, 1974.

May, George S., ed. *The Automobile Industry, 1920–1980.* Facts on File, 1989.

Morgan, Robert P. *Twentieth-Century Music: A History of Musical Style in Modern Europe and America.* Norton, 1991.

Noble, David W., David A. Horowitz, and Peter N. Carroll. *Twentieth Century Limited: A History of Recent America.* Houghton Mifflin, 1980.

Norman, Philip. *The Road Goes On Forever: Portraits from a Journey Through Contemporary Music.* Simon & Schuster, 1982.

Olderman, Murray. *Nelson's Twentieth Century Encyclopedia of Baseball.* Nelson, 1963.

Oliver, John W. *History of American Technology.* Books on Demand UMI, 1956.

Ritter, Lawrence S. *The Story of Baseball.* Morrow, 1983.

Sklar, Robert. *Movie-Made America: A Cultural History of American Movies.* Random House, 1976.

Spaeth, Sigmund. *A History of Popular Music in America.* Random House, 1948.

Susman, Warren I. *Culture as History: The Transformation of American Society in the Twentieth Century.* Pantheon, 1984.

Taft, Philip. *Organized Labor in American History.* Harper & Row, 1964.

Vecsey, George, ed. *The Way It Was: Great Sports Events from the Past.* McGraw-Hill, 1974.

Zinn, Howard. *The Twentieth Century: A People's History.* Harper & Row, 1984.

About the Era

Bernstein, Carl, and Bob Woodward. *All the President's Men.* Simon & Schuster, 1974.

Branch, Taylor. *Parting the Waters: America in the King Years, 1954–1963.* Simon & Schuster, 1989.

Carroll, Peter. *It Seemed Like Nothing Happened: The Tragedy and Promise of America in the 1970s.* Rutgers University Press, 1990.

Cook, Fred J. *The Crimes of Watergate.* Franklin Watts, 1981.

Emmens, Carol A. *An Album of the Sixties.* Franklin Watts, 1981.

Fitzgerald, Frances. *Fire in the Lake: The Vietnamese and the Americans in Vietnam.* Random House, 1973.

Freeman, Jo, ed. *Social Movements of the Sixties and Seventies.* Longman, 1983.

Friedan, Betty. *The Feminine Mystique.* Dell, 1975.

Gitlin, Todd. *The Sixties: Years of Hope, Days of Rage.* Bantam, 1989.

Halberstam, David. *The Best and the Brightest.* Random House, 1972.

Hampton, Henry, and Steve Fayer, with Sarah Flynn. *Voices of Freedom: An Oral History of the Civil Rights Movement from the 1950s through the 1980s.* Bantam, 1990.

Hendler, Herb. *Year by Year in the Rock Era: Events and Conditions Shaping the Rock Generation That Reshaped America.* Greenwood Press, 1983.

Hoobler, Dorothy, and Thomas Hoobler. *An Album of the Seventies.* Franklin Watts, 1981.

Karnow, Stanley. *Vietnam: A History.* Viking, 1983.

King, Coretta Scott, ed. *The Words of Martin Luther King, Jr.* Newmarket, 1983.

Morris, Charles R. *Time of Passion: America, 1960–1980.* Harper & Row, 1984.

Powledge, Fred. *Free at Last? The Civil Rights Movement and the People Who Made It.* Little, Brown, 1990.

Reedy, George E. *Lyndon B. Johnson: A Memoir.* Andrews & McMeel, 1982.

Safire, William. *Before the Fall: An Inside View of the Pre-Watergate White House.* Doubleday, 1975.

Schell, Jonathan. *The Time of Illusion.* Random House, 1976.

Wheen, Francis. *The Sixties: A Fresh Look at a Decade of Change.* Century Publishing, 1982.

White, Theodore H. *The Making of a President, 1960.* Macmillan, 1989.

Wolfe, Tom. *The Right Stuff.* Bantam, 1983.

Wright, Lawrence. *In the New World: Growing Up with America from the Sixties to the Eighties.* Random House, 1989.

Index